HOUNDS
OF THE WORLD

HOUNDS OF THE WORLD

AN ILLUSTRATED GUIDE

DAVID ALDERTON

Photography by Bruce Tanner

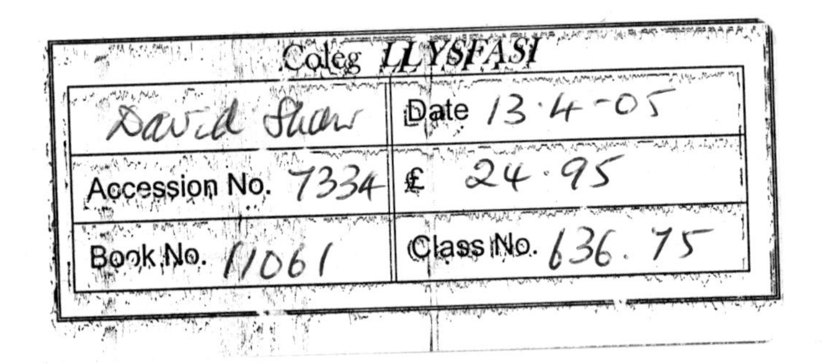

First published in the UK in 2000
by Swan Hill Press, an imprint of Airlife Publishing Ltd

British Library Cataloguing-in-Publication Data
A catalogue record for this book
is available from the British Library

ISBN 1 85310 912 6

Typeset by Servis Filmsetting Ltd, Manchester, England
Printed in Italy

Swan Hill Press
an imprint of Airlife Publishing Ltd
101 Longden Road, Shrewsbury, SY3 9EB, England
E-mail: airlife@airlifebooks.com
Website: www.airlifebooks.com

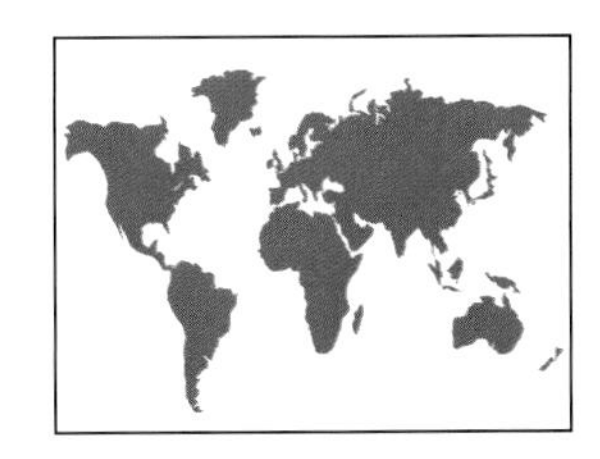

ACKNOWLEDGEMENTS

It is easy to overlook the fact that a book of this type, where all the photographs are specially taken, can only be accomplished with the help and generosity of many people. On our travels, we were lucky enough to encounter a host of fellow canine enthusiasts, who made it possible.

Particular thanks for photographic assistance are due to Denise Palmer, Manon Droz and Sarah Maher, as well as Rita Hemsley for typing the manuscript.

The following people kindly helped with photographic contacts and tracking down particular hounds:

Renate Aller, London, England
Ann Aslett, Walthamstow Stadium, London, England
Anthony Bongiovanni, Bridgwater, Somerset, England
Manon Droz, London, England
Georg Henning, Marburg, Germany
Kristine Lampman, Lampman Kennels, Wellandport, Ontario, Canada
Hilary Murphy, Blindley Heath Afghan Racing, England
Dave Neihaus, Baldwin, Illinois, USA
Vivien Phillips, Berkhamsted, Hertfordshire, England
Shirley Rawlings, Secretary, Hound Association, Derbyshire, England
Société Canine de Normandie, Elbeuf, France
Jenny Startup, Baldock, Hertfordshire, England

Many thanks are also due to the following dog owners/breeders and others who assisted directly with the photographs of the hounds featured in this book, but are not named individually:

England
Albany Bassetts, Renate Aller, Diana Berry, Anthony Bongiovanni, L. Johnson, Merymut Pharoah Hounds, Moira Millerick, Mimi and Evangelos, Peter Palmer, Vivien Phillips, Shirley Rawlings, Jenny Startup

Canada
Jim and Kristine Lampman, Bob Anderson, Dave Broath, John and Moya Quinton

France
Guy Gaudfroy, members of the Société Canine de Normandie and exhibitors at their Dieppe show

Germany
Manfred Fischer, Georg Henning, Christina Pfeiffer, Gregor Weitzel

USA
Carl Brandenburger Jr, Dennis Van Buren, Mary Hislop, Rod Huber, Larry Kempfer, Jay Kern, Rick Marshall, Myron Neff, Bill Odle, Ron Sinn

David Alderton and Bruce Tanner

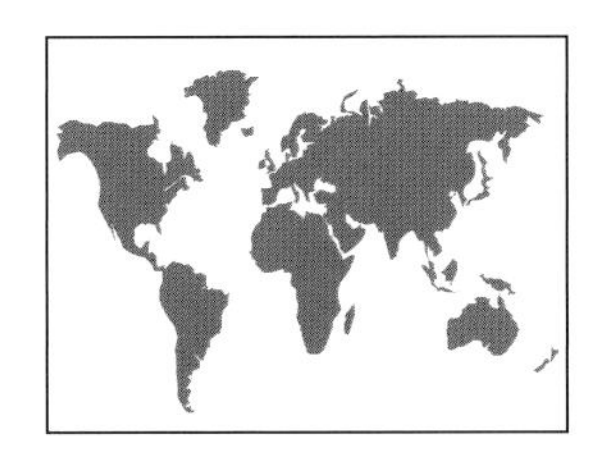

CONTENTS

Chapter numbers are shown within brackets on the map

Switzerland (6)
Berner laufhund
Berner neiderlaufhund
Jura laufhund: bruno
Jura laufhund: St. Hubert
Luzerner laufhund
Luzerner neiderlaufhund
Schweizer laufhund
Schweizer neiderlaufhund
Canada (7)
Tahltan bear dog
Canary Islands (2)
Canary Islands hound (2)
Ireland (5)
Irish wolfhound
Kerry beagle
Norway (6)
Dunker
Haldenstovare
Hygenhund
Canada
Great Britain
Ireland
Spain
Portugal
Morocco
Canary Islands
United States
USA (7)
American black & tan coonhound
American blue Gascon hound
American foxhound
Black mouth cur
Blue tick coonhound
Catahoula leopard dog
English coonhound
Leopard cur
Majestic tree hound
Plott hound
Redbone coonhound
Stephens cur
Treeing Tennessee brindle
Treeing walker coonhound
Morocco (2)
Sloughi
Mali
Mali (2)
Azawakh
Congo (2)
Basenji
France (5)
Anglo-Francais
Ariégeois
Basset Artésian Normand
Basset bleu de Gascogne
Basset fauve de Bretagne
Beagle harrier
Billy
Briquet griffon Vendéen
Chien d'Artois
Francais Tricolores
Grand basset griffon Vendéen
Grand bleu de Gascogne
Grand Gascon-Saintongeois
Grand griffon Vendéen
Griffon fauve de Bretagne
Griffon Nivernais
Petit basset griffon Vendéen
Petit bleu de Gascogne
Petit Gascon-Saintongeois
Petit griffon bleu de Gascogne
Poitevin
Porcelaine
Brazil
Argentina (7)
Dogo Argentino
Portugal (2)
Portuguese podengo :
grande/medio/pequeno
Argentina
Germany (6)
Deutsche bracke
Bavarian schweisshund
Hanoverian schweisshund
Miniature dachshund
Standard dachshund
Westphalian dachsbracke
Brazil (7)
Fila Brasileiro
Rastreador Brasileiro
Great Britain (5)
Basset hound
Beagle
Bloodhound
Deerhound
Fell hound
Foxhound
Greyhound
Harrier
Italian greyhound
Longdog
Lurcher
Otterhound
Staghound
Welsh foxhound
Whippet

Sweden (6)
Drever
Hamiltonstövare
Schillerstövare
Smalandsstövare
Finland (6)
Finnish hound
Denmark (6)
trellufstover
Austria (6)
Alpenlandischer dachsbracke
Austrian brandlbracke
Peintinger bracke
Tyroler bracke
Poland (6)
Polish hound
Slovakia (6)
Slovakian hound
Estonia (6)
Gontchaja Estonskaja
Latvia (6)
Latvian hound
Lithuania (6)
Lithuanian hound
Hungary (6)
Hungarian greyhound
Transylvanian hound
Russia (6)
Borzois
Chortaj
Russian harlequin hound
Russian drab yellow hound
Tasy
Sweden
Finland
Estonia
Latvia
Lithuania
Poland
ustria
Slovakia
Hungary
Yugoslavia
icily
Greece
Malta & Gozo
Russia
Afghanistan
Arabia
India
Thailand
Congo
Zimbabwe
Australia
Greece (6)
Greek greyhound
Hellenic hound
Italy (2)
Italian hound
Afghanistan (6)
Afghan hound
India (6)
Banjara greyhound
Mahratta greyhound
Rampur greyhound
Arabia (2)
Saluki
Thailand (6)
Thai ridgeback
Majorca (2)
Mallorquin
Ibiza (2)
Ibizan hound
Sicily (2)
Sicilian hound
Malta & Gozo (2)
Pharaoh hound
Yugoslavia (former)(6)
Balksenski gonic
Bosnian rough-haired hound
Istrian hounds: resasti & kratkodlaki
Posavski gonic
Yugoslavian mountain hound
Yugoslavian tricoloured hound
Spain (2)
Sabueso Espanol de Monte
Sabueso Espanol Lebrero
Spanish greyhound
Zimbabwe (2)
Rhodesian ridgeback
Australia (6)
Kangaroo hound

Many aspects of the behaviour of grey wolves can be seen in the case of hounds, not the least their pack structure, but there are also differences. Scenthounds, for example, are actually far more ready to give voice than their wild ancestors.

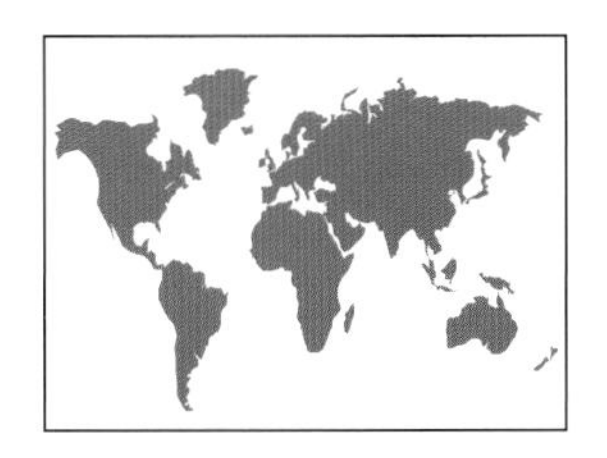

CHAPTER 1
IN THE BEGINNING

Current scientific investigations are now pushing the origins of the domestic dog back far beyond the archaeological evidence which has been unearthed to date. The latest research, relying on DNA fingerprinting, suggests that the relationship between people and dogs could extend back over 100,000 years.

Early human settlements were scattered over a wide area and the first contact between people and wolves in such surroundings is believed to have been haphazard. Wolf cubs may have been brought back and reared in the settlement. They would have lost some of their natural shyness at that stage and would have stayed where food was available. In times of hardship however, the tables were certainly turned with the result that the wolves themselves would have been used as a source of food. Horrific as it appears to western sensibilities, the consumption of dogs continues even today in some parts of Asia.

A study of the origins of today's breeds closely parallels the former distribution of the grey wolf (*Canis lupus*). It is no coincidence that the vast majority of breeds have their origins north of the equator, where the grey wolf used to be the most widely-distributed of the larger mammals.

These breeds are often grouped today on similarities in appearance, suggesting that each group was derived from a common ancestor. As examples, the large mastiff breeds are believed to be descended from Asiatic wolves and the spitz breeds from wolves of the far north, while the earliest hounds trace their origins back to the vicinity of the Middle East.

The differences that are apparent between the breeds of today can be traced back to variations in the appearance of wolves in different parts of their huge range. In the far north of Alaska, the largest wolves in the world are to be found, relying on their combined strength to overcome strong and potentially dangerous quarry, such as moose.

Middle Eastern populations of the grey wolf differ significantly however, being smaller in size and tending to have paler sandy-coloured coats. Fleet of foot, these wolves are dependent on their pace to hunt, running down creatures such as gazelles, in areas where natural cover to ambush prey is not readily available.

It is not surprising that the dogs developed from these wolves shared similar characteristics with their ancestors, just as those breeds from the far north of America, such as the Alaskan malamute, are immensely powerful and invaluable as sled dogs.

Domestication of the dog therefore almost certainly took place at various localities and times in history. Insight into how the early proto-dogs behaved has been derived in part from a breeding project which was undertaken by a Dutchman called Leendert Saarloos. During the 1930s, he sought to reinvigorate the German shepherd dog (or Alsatian, as it has sometimes been known), believing it to have become genetically weakened as a result of inbreeding down the centuries.

Saarloos therefore began by attempting to breed a German shepherd dog and grey wolf together, but the wolf died as the result of viral illness which was believed to have been contracted from the dog. Nevertheless, Saarloos was undeterred and the first generation puppies that finally resulted from this crossing proved to be far more nervous of contact with people than those of pure domestic dogs. In addition, they also displayed strong pack instincts and they did not prove responsive to training, compared with ordinary dogs.

Saarloos's breeding programme only involved a single wolf cross at the outset, and although not common today, the resulting breed that bears his name – the Saarloos wolfhound – is to be seen in small numbers at shows in continental Europe.

Borzoi puppy and owner. Today, hounds are widely kept as companions, rather than for their hunting prowess.

Treeing Walker coonhound. One of a number of breeds developed in North America, whose ancestors were taken there as the result of European settlement.

It is not easy to pinpoint the exact period in history when wolves actually became dogs. This depends largely on archaeological evidence, which reflects the skeletal changes that have taken place, but unfortunately relatively few complete skeletons of early dogs have been unearthed.

Study of the structure of the skull is especially significant, with the ancient sighthound lineage, as typified by the greyhound, having an elongated and narrowed nasal area, compared with that of the wolf. Even so, this factor has perhaps been overstressed in the past, given that studies involving European grey wolves have revealed that the cranial anatomy of their offspring is variable, even within the same litter.

There can be cubs with short, compacted brachycephalic skulls, while others range from medium length (mesocephalic) through to the elongated shape associated with sighthounds, and described as dolichocephalic. Less obvious, but of no less significance in assessing the emergence of the domestic dog is a reduction in the size of the teeth, coupled with weaker jaws, as reflected by the area of attachment for the muscles here.

These features together suggest that the early hounds were generally employed more to harry their quarry than kill it. The actual positioning of the teeth also differs, with the pre-molars (located behind the pointed canine teeth in each jaw) no longer overlapping in domestic dogs, in contrast with their wolf ancestor.

It is the Arabian subspecies of the grey wolf, known scientifically as *Canis lupus pallipes*, found across the Arabian peninsula and extending to Iraq, India and Pakistan, which is considered as the most likely ancestor of the hound lineage. Sadly, it is now in danger of extinction in many parts of its range, with current estimates suggesting that there are less than 300 individuals of this subspecies to be found on the Arabian peninsula itself.

The earliest actual physical evidence of the presence of hound-type dogs dates back to the end of the pre-dynastic period in Egypt, about 5 thousand years ago. The portrayals of dogs on artifacts such as bowls and in the form of rock

There are still dogs which represent an intermediate stage in the domestication process, such as the New Guinea singing dog, so called because of its distinctive call. It is related to the Australian dingo.

drawings also provides further evidence that the domestication process was underway by this stage. They show hunters armed with bows and arrows, being clearly assisted by dogs, in the pursuit of quarry such as Barbary sheep.

Although it is hard to draw significant conclusions about the appearance of the dogs, there is no doubt that in contrast to wild wolves, they are characterised by their raised tails. These primitive drawings, portraying hunting dogs, represent some of the very earliest portrayals of hounds in action.

Other early rock drawings from this part of the world show a dog not dissimilar in profile to a greyhound harrying an ostrich, which the hunter is shooting with an arrow. This is a highly significant piece of rock art, confirming the value of having a dog that was capable of pursuing fast-moving quarry. Ostriches can attain speeds of 65 kph and they are capable of lashing out with their powerful feet, making them formidable adversaries.

It is not hard to imagine how people at that stage in history came to prize the most agile, fleet-footed hunting dogs, and the very best would have been preferred for breeding purposes. As a result, a recognisable strain – similar to our definition of a breed – evolved, with such dogs being kept essentially for their hunting prowess.

The cave paintings reveal that there were other types of dog in existence at the same time, confirming the value of these early hounds in the context of human society. It is no coincidence that, subsequently, the keeping of hounds became closely linked with the ruling class, whether among the nomadic tribespeople of Africa or the royal courts in France or Britain.

Hounds, probably more than any other group of dogs, have matured with us and influenced our lifestyles right down to the present day. Even when it was no longer essential to hunt to place meat on the table, hounds maintained their following in a more leisured society. They were taken on the voyages of colonisation to the New World and Australia, adapting once again to these new environments and soon evolving further in such surroundings. More recently, they have also moved into our homes simply as companions and entered the show ring, while still retaining their athletic poise.

Hounds have never entirely sacrificed their independence or nobility of spirit, and although frustrating on occasions, these characteristics are undeniably part of their appeal. Simply surrendering to our whims is not their intent. Obedience training is made correspondingly difficult in most cases as a result, but their amiable and friendly natures provide real compensation for such shortcomings. Owning a hound is not like keeping a passive pet – instead, it is about having a true companion who may choose on occasions to disagree with your aims, but does so without any hint of malice or lasting resentment!

LEFT: Smaller hounds are favoured as pets today, such as dachshunds like this smooth-coated individual.

BELOW: The whippet has a reputation as a highly affectionate hound, and is bred in a wide range of colour forms.

RIGHT: The elongated, narrow nose of the greyhound, seen here in profile, reveals that it is a member of the sighthound group

BELOW LEFT: The Grand Bleu de Gascogne displays the typical profile of a scenthound, with a large nose, pendant lips and large, low-set ears. The mottling varies in intensity between individuals, but the light tan markings above the eyes are a consistent feature.

BOTTOM: A treeing Walker coonhound. The markings of hounds are unique, often enabling individuals to be distinguished from some distance away.

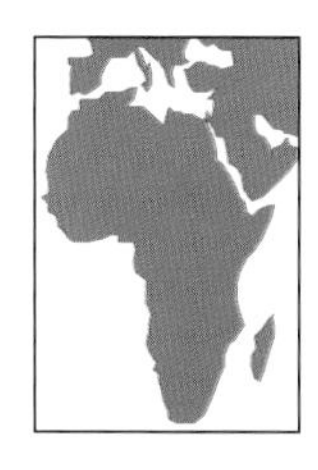

Chapter 2
The Hounds of the Mediterranean and Africa

The Mediterranean region was the birthplace of the hound lineage, and the ancestral links remain very clear in this region today, from the breeds represented there. Sighthounds predominate, following a tradition dating back over thousands of years. Many, such as the Pharaoh hound, bear a striking resemblance to the Egyptian god Anubis, responsible for assisting the souls of the departed into the after life.

These hounds had been highly prized, with an ancient inscription found at Giza revealing that one of their kind called Abuwtiyuw had been buried with great ceremony by order of the kings. This suggests that such breeds have changed little for thousands of years and represent a distinctive group, especially since hounds of similar appearance have not evolved elsewhere in the world. Their prick-ears are unique.

The Pharaoh hound is a distinctive shade of tan, often with a small white area in the vicinity of the lower throat, which is known as the star.

The ear cartilage of the Pharaoh hound is very flexible at the base, and only when alert will the hound raise its ears.

The Phoenicians were probably responsible for the distribution of the breeds seen today, having plied their trade around the Mediterranean region by ship since about 3000 BC. This helps to explain the presence of such hounds on various Mediterranean islands, such as Sicily and Malta.

Having originated in Egypt about 4,000 years ago, the Pharaoh hound ultimately died out in its homeland but its descendants thrived on the islands of Malta and nearby Gozo. Here they remained essentially unknown to the outside world until the late 1960s, when a group of these hounds was imported to Britain. Their striking looks, attractive coloration and friendly character meant that they soon built up an international following.

Although slightly smaller in size, the Sicilian hound is very similar in appearance to the Pharaoh hound. It originates further north in the Mediterranean, on the island of Sicily where it is known locally as Cirneco dell'Etna, having hunted on the slopes of the Mount Etna volcano for up to 3,000 years when its ancestors are believed to have been brought to the island.

This Pharaoh hound is seeking to track the source of a sound, having only one of its ears directed forwards.

The Ibizan hound has extensive white areas on its coat which help to distinguish it from the Pharaoh hound.

As in the case of similar breeds, the Sicilian hound is predominantly a sighthound, but can also hunt by scent, reflecting its versatility. Agile by nature, these hounds are adept at pursuing rabbits and hares even over steep, uneven surfaces.

The rough-coated form of the Ibizan hound tends to be less popular than its sleek, smooth-haired counterpart.

Another descendant of the ancient Egyptian hounds is to be found to the west, within the Balearic group of islands off the eastern coast of Spain, on the island of Ibiza. The Ibizan hound is the tallest of the prick-eared hounds, also occurring in both a rough and long-coated form although its coloration does not differ significantly from that of other members of the group. It is also sometimes described as the Podenco Ibicenco. The breed's ancestors were almost certainly brought to Ibiza following the Roman invasion of Egypt in the 9th century BC, which forced many Phoenicians to flee to this island.

In turn, some Ibizan hounds were taken to the Spanish mainland and here the breed formed the basis for the Spanish greyhound (Galgo Español) at an early stage in history. This breed marks a divergence in type however, from the Egyptian hound lineage, not least because of its pendulous, rose-shaped ears. It is likely to have been evolved from crossings between the Ibizan hound and the sloughi from North Africa (see page 26).

The Spanish greyhound is smaller in size than the English form, which has also been involved in its development, especially during recent times. The existence of a wire-haired form is a reflection of the contribution from the Ibizan hound, as is its broader, shorter muzzle, compared with the English greyhound. Temperamentally however, the Galgo Español is somewhat shyer, especially of strangers, which is a characteristic associated with the North African breeds. It is faster than the Ibizan hound, able to sprint at speeds of 30mph (48kph) in pursuit of its quarry, although in recent times, Spanish greyhounds have become much more popular as show rather than hunting dogs.

A breed which is effectively identical to the Ibizan hound is the Mallorquin, which is confined to the neighbouring island of Mallorca (Majorca), being unrecognised in its own right elsewhere. As with its better-known relatives, these hounds are exceedingly versatile, hunting both in packs or singly, and also being trained on occasions to work as retrievers.

On the Canary Islands, through the Straits of Gibraltar and just off the western coast of North Africa, the indigenous hounds hunt rabbits, scenting them with their keen noses and driving them out from their hiding places in stone walls. These hounds are also of Egyptian origin but can be distinguished from other breeds by their curled tails. They are apparently unknown outside these islands.

The versatility of the Mediterranean hounds is probably most apparent today in the case of the Portuguese hound, also called the Portuguese Podengo. It occurs in three distinct sizes, each of which operate in a different way. The largest form shows a very distinctive similarity in appearance to the Ibizan hound, attaining a broadly equivalent height and often displaying the same coloration. This Grande form is a sighthound with good pace, able to chase deer across open countryside, as well as rabbits. Even in the short-coated form however, these hounds have a longer, coarser coat than those from the Mediterranean. There is also a wire-coated variant more common in upland areas, again suggestive of a link with the Ibizan hound, which is reinforced by the prick-eared appearance of these Portuguese hounds.

A characteristic of these hounds is that instead

Ibizan hounds are less specialised than hound breeds of more recent origins, hunting by a combination of sight and scent.

Segugio Italiano. The influence of northern hunting dogs can be seen here, particularly in terms of the long, pendulous ears.

of being glossy and moist, their noses often appear to be dry. It is believed that this feature may handicap their scenting skills, but conversely, their vision is certainly more acute than that of scenthounds. The light coloured iris surrounding the pupil is thought to be linked with keen vision, while the oval shape of the eye itself may help them to see well even under conditions of bright sunlight and can serve to keep dust out of the eyes in dry terrain.

The Medio Podengo Portugueso is in effect a smaller version of the Grande, and not as fleet of foot, due in part to its shorter legs, but usually proves to be more agile. It is kept primarily as a hound, chasing rabbits and hares, whereas the Grande form is also valued as a watchdog. Again, a wire-haired form is known.

The smallest form of the Podengo Portugueso is rather different in appearance from its larger relatives. The smooth-coated version in particular looks rather similar at first glance to a chihuahua, thanks to its pricked ears, although its head is not as rounded. The Pequeño is traditionally used as a terrier, with its small size allowing it to disappear down rabbit burrows and drive the occupants up above ground, so they can be shot or coursed by the Pequeño's larger relatives. Their terrier-like instincts extend to rat killing, for which they are highly valued.

Ranking among the smallest hounds in the world, it is perhaps not surprising that in recent years, the Pequeño Podengo Portugueso has become increasingly popular outside its homeland as a companion dog.

The Segugio Italiano or Italian hound probably represents a fusion of the ancient Egyptian hounds and European scenthounds of bloodhound type, notably the Celtic hound, as manifested by the breed's low-set pendulous ears. It retains a more athletic build however, reminiscent of sighthounds, with a slightly roached (convex-shaped) back, falling away over the hindquarters.

The head shape, and particularly the breadth of the nose, indicates that the Segugio Italiano is a scenthound.

Italian hounds have a justified reputation as versatile hunters, although today they tend to be used mainly against rabbits and hares. These hounds were highly prized during the Renaissance era in Italy, taking part in elaborate hunts, accompanied by riders on horseback and a retinue of hunt servants.

The breed has undergone a renaissance of its own in recent times, both in its homeland and elsewhere in the world, becoming more widely kept as individuals rather than pack hounds. These are not dogs for the faint-hearted however; Segugio Italianos traditionally display considerable stamina when hunting, often staying in the field for twelve hours or so without a break. Their thin curved tails are carried high, resembling a sabre in shape, and enable these hounds to be spotted easily, even in undergrowth, with their scenthound ancestry being revealed at this stage by their baying calls. They have changed little in appearance for over a thousand years, as revealed by statues such as *Diana the Huntress* which can be seen at the Naples Museum and portrays an unmistakable image of this breed.

Two coat types are recognised. The Segugio Italiano a Pelo Raso is the smooth-coated variant, which has a very sleek, muscular appearance, while the rough-haired form, known as the Segugio Italiano a Pelo Forte looks a markedly different hound. It has bushy eyebrows and a rough, tousled coat and may have originally been favoured for hunting in cooler, mountainous areas. This combination of both smooth and rough-coated examples of the same breed is not unique however; it is a feature associated with a number of other breeds of hound, including the Podengo Portugueso and various French hounds. In terms of temperament, the Segugio Italiano is a typical hound – friendly and lively by nature, with a somewhat stubborn streak which is likely to be manifested during obedience training.

The Spanish hound may itself have contributed to the development of its Italian relative, being introduced to Spain by the Celts at an early stage in history. Known in its homeland as the Sabueso

Seen in profile, it is clear that the ears are low-set in the Segugio Italiano, at a level just below that of the eyes.

Español, it has not altered significantly in appearance over the centuries, showing the characteristic features associated with the Celtic and subsequent St Hubert hound lineage. The nose is broad and the head is long, with the forehead being wrinkled. The pendulous ears are set well back and the dewlap is prominent, as are the flews. The body is muscular with the tail being low set and tapering along its length.

Two separate varieties of Sabueso Español are recognised, both of which are smooth-coated. They are distinguished on grounds of size, with the large Spanish hound, or Sabueso Español de Monte also showing more variable coloration than its smaller relative. The Sabueso Español Lebrero has essentially solid coloration, with greatly reduced areas of white hair. These tend to be confined to a blaze on the face, the lower area of the neck extending over the chest and belly. White markings on the paws and at the tip of the tail are also quite characteristic.

Sabueso Españoles were formerly kept for hunting in packs, but today they are used more widely for police work, where their scenting skills can be invaluable for tracking purposes, following trails that have long become cold. They work well on an individual basis with a handler, but their active natures and considerable stamina mean the breed is not suitable as a typical household companion, in spite of its affectionate nature. Relatively few Sabueso Españoles are kept outside their homeland, where the Lebrero form has now become very scarce.

Across the Mediterranean Sea, in North Africa, are several other representatives of the sighthound group, whose ancestry may be traced back to ancient Egypt or possibly even earlier in the case of the saluki. Its name probably originates from the ancient city of Saluki, in southern Arabia. An ivory head of a dog clearly resembling the saluki, wearing a collar, dating back nearly 7,000 years, is one of the oldest representations of any domestic dog. There is also a painting found at Hierakonapolis, thought to have been executed about 3600 BC, again portraying a hound which is very similar in appearance to a modern saluki.

The saluki – one of the natural athletes of the canine world. Their forelimbs are long and straight.

The gentle, noble expression of the saluki owes much to its eyes. These are large and oval, and usually dark in colour.

Fennec fox – a wild canid which is equipped to survive in the heat of the desert, sharing characteristics with the saluki.

The prowess of such hounds in running down and overpowering gazelles – fast, agile members of the antelope family – was highly prized at an early stage in history. Greek writers accompanying the army of Xenophon admired their ability to overtake their quarry without human intervention. There is even a suggestion that the breed may alternatively have been named after the town of Seleukia in Syria, at the time when this region formed part of the Greek Empire.

The desert-dwelling Bedouin people referred to the saluki as *El Hor*, meaning 'the noble one', sometimes pitching these hounds against gazelles with a hawk flying overhead to harry the antelope. Speed was considered vital in the desert, whether it was the athletic saluki or the fast Arabian horse. The Bedouin valued the pedigree of their hounds, and although the ancestral tree was never recorded in writing, it was passed down the generations, forming an integral part of their culture.

So treasured were these hounds that they were never sold, but they would be given as gifts, or in return for assistance. Salukis are predominantly smooth-coated, helping them to stay cool under the hot sun, with the longer fur between their toes being an aid to prevent them from sinking into the desert and keeping them cool. A similar adaptation is seen in the case of the fennec fox (*Fennecus zerda*), a wild canid occurring in the same area.

The ears were traditionally cropped (cut) in puppyhood, to prevent the long silky hair from becoming matted, which could lead to infection. Although not as fast as a greyhound, the saluki has much greater stamina, often being required to run for over 3 miles (4.8km) in pursuit of its quarry. Puppies were traditionally reared by the Bedouin women, with early training beginning when the young hounds were roughly four months old.

The colour variants that exist in the saluki today used to have a regional significance. Lighter shades such as white and cream were commonly seen in what was Mesopotamia, with the dark colours, notably the black and tan, originating from the upland areas of Syria. Fawn and red salukis were more likely to be encountered further south, in what is now Saudi Arabia.

This saluki is tricoloured, but these hounds can vary in colour from shades of cream through fawn to black-and-tan.

The earliest European contact with the saluki was probably during the Crusades, perhaps in the 12th century. There is a French tapestry portraying salukis in the entourage of the English King Richard I (1189–99), who was also known as Richard the Lionheart.

Salukis were subsequently introduced to Britain in recent times by the Hon. Florence Amherst in 1897, after she had been presented with a pair of young puppies. The breed was finally recognised by the Kennel Club during 1922, with a specialist breed club being founded the following year. Salukis from Britain were then taken to the USA, where the American Kennel Club accepted the breed in 1927. Other specimens, obtained in various parts of the Middle East, were subsequently used in the breeding programme of Esther Bliss Knapp in Ohio during the 1930s, which formed the basis of her Pine Paddock Kennels bloodline.

Although today, the saluki is effectively standardised, local variants have been well-documented, with sixteen being described from its homeland. In fact the first examples of the breed obtained by the Hon. Florence Amherst from Arabia were smaller, with less developed feathering on their legs than those of Persian ancestry. Although not bred in large numbers, the long-coated saluki is seen occasionally, even today.

The head of the saluki is naturally held high, and is long and narrow in shape, as befits a sighthound.

The saluki has been mistakenly confused with a closely-related smooth-coated breed called the sloughi, whose homeland lies further west in North Africa. Images of hounds of this type have been found on rocks from the Neolithic period, possibly extending back over 8,000 years. Morocco has now assumed the mantle for the birthplace of the sloughi, which is also sometimes described as the Arabian greyhound. Those originating from the vicinity of the Atlas Mountains tend to be slightly larger in size and brindle in appearance, whereas those from the desert region are yellowish.

Sloughis have been highly-prized down the millennia, both for hunting purposes and as loyal guardians. The birth of a litter is traditionally a cause for celebration, while following the death of a cherished sloughi, guests bring traditional offerings of lamb and sugar, to commemorate its passing. In common with the saluki, these hounds are not regarded in this Muslim region as being unclean, in contrast to the pariah dogs which are also found there. Their loyalty develops early in life, and is unswerving, although in the company of strangers, a sloughi may appear to display a rather reserved and uncommunicative nature.

It is certainly not a typical greyhound, possessing a gait which is more akin to that of the Afghan hound. Both breeds have short hocks, which provides them with great control and manoeuvrability, enabling quarry to be closely pursued at speed, even if it twists and turns in an attempt to throw the sloughi off its trail. Rabbits and gazelles are typically hunted with these hounds. Although not considered to be quite as fast as a saluki, the sloughi is regarded as being better at running down its quarry, thanks in part to its broader muzzle and surer but smaller feet.

The breed was probably first brought to Europe at an early stage in history, since Hannibal the Great crossed the Alps in 218 BC with a detachment of Berber cavalry from North Africa, who are likely to have brought their hounds with them. As mentioned previously (see pages 19–20), the breed has left its mark in Europe, contributing to the development of the Spanish greyhound in the past.

It was reported to have been a favoured breed of the Egyptian ruler Tutankhamen, with portrayals of it being associated with his tomb. Although there is no evidence of a long-haired variant, there are records of British officers keeping sloughis with pricked rather than drop ears during the 1920s in what was then Palestine. These particular hounds are believed to have originated from Egypt.

The breed attracted great interest when three examples of these hounds were brought to the Netherlands in 1898, providing inspiration for the artist August Legras. It is easily distinguished by the presence of darker hair, forming so-called spectacles around its characteristic large, dark eyes. Some sloughis also have an accompanying black mask, plus a so-called black 'manteau', or saddle area on the back.

Many sloughis were imported to France from its former North African colony Algeria, but the breed is certainly not common, either in Europe or North America, although it can often be seen in small numbers at the bigger shows. A young sloughi must have careful training, to prevent it from outrunning and overpowering small dogs and cats. They are brave hunters, with three-year-old sloughis traditionally being expected to run down wild boar, which make formidable and dangerous adversaries.

Sloughi. Some, but not all examples of this breed have a black facial mask, as shown in the case of this individual.

The third member of the North African group of sighthounds is sometimes called the Tuareg sloughi, but is better known now as the Azawakh. This breed is native to Mali, where it has been evolved by the Tuareg nomads. These hounds are exceedingly slender in build, carrying no fat on their bodies, to the extent that their ribs are normally visible. The head is domed and pear-shaped, with their coloration being shades of fawn, ranging to dark red, offset against white markings, typically on the chest and underparts.

ABOVE: Regional differences can be detected in sloughi stock. Those of desert descent are lighter-boned than those bred to hunt in mountainous areas.

BELOW: The ears of the sloughi are relatively flat and triangular in shape, with rounded tips.

Azawakhs were first bred over 1,000 years ago and they are not only kept for hunting, but also for guarding precious livestock such as goats against predators including hyaenas and jackals. The presence of white markings on their hounds is regarded as essential by the Tuareg, as are five distinctive wart-like swellings on the face, the most obvious of which are located below the eyes.

Azawakhs are natural athletes, with long, powerful legs and a deep-chested body. The Tuareg have traditionally selected only the very best male puppy from each litter, and occasionally a young bitch, before culling the other puppies. They are reared entirely on milk, and initially encouraged to hunt rats, before progressing to hares and larger game. When the Tuareg go hunting, the Azawakhs travel with them, being carried on their camels. Once quarry is spotted, the hounds are released and during the chase, an Azawakh can attain a speed of more than 40mph (64kph), hunting entirely by sight.

The breed also displays considerable stamina, with chases sometimes lasting for over five hours under the hot African sun. Having caught its quarry, the Azawakh holds the unfortunate animal until it can be killed, rather than undertaking this task itself.

The Azawakh has a very short, fine coat, as befits a breed from a desert region. Its head resembles a pear in shape.

The deep chest and athletic build of the Azawakh give these hounds considerable stamina as well as pace.

The importance of these hounds in the Tuareg culture is such that without them, these people would have no effective means of catching gazelles and similar game. Not surprisingly therefore, the Azawakh was, and still is, highly prized. For many years it was impossible for outsiders to acquire any of these hounds. The breed represents probably the least modified sighthound lineage, having been so preciously guarded by its creators.

It was thanks to the Yugoslav ambassador to the Upper Volta and Ivory Coast that the Azawakh was finally introduced to Europe. Dr Pecar tried over the course of many years to persuade the Tuareg to part with a couple of their hounds, but without success. Then on his return home, he was awarded a male dog, having gained the respect of the Tuareg as a hunter. When he came back to Africa, he was called upon to kill a rogue elephant, which had been attacking people. On this occasion, the Tuareg presented Dr Pecar with a starving bitch, which he successfully nursed back to health, and so was able to begin breeding these sighthounds in Europe.

Although still not common, Azawakhs are seen in small numbers at major shows, being most numerous today in Germany and increasingly in France. The breed was recognised by the Fédération Cynologique International (FCI) in 1980.

The nature of the Azawakh is such that it has specific requirements, requiring plenty of exercise to keep fit. It runs in a relatively effortless style that has been compared with that of another desert athlete, the Arab horse. Its body length is quite short, from the point of the shoulder to the hips, compared with the length of its legs, while the deep chest provides good lung capacity.

The Azawakh also has an independent streak which can cause problems during training. The short, thin coat may be all that is required in the desert, but in more temperate climates, combined with the lack of body fat, these hounds do feel the cold and should be protected accordingly with a coat. It is normal for their ribs to be discernible, and unfortunately the elegance of the breed will soon be lost by overfeeding, especially if combined with a lack of opportunity to exercise. As with many hounds, Azawakhs will not hesitate to steal food if the opportunity presents itself, and this too will contribute to obesity. Weighing these hounds regularly is therefore recommended.

Occurring further south in Africa is another dog which has remained essentially unknown outside its native area until comparatively recently. The basenji does not share a common ancestry with the Egyptian sighthounds however, although it was apparently known at this early stage in history. This highly unusual breed is descended from the pariah dogs of the region. Its distribution used to be based in the former area of the Congo which is why it is sometimes called the Congo dog. The breed has a relatively short jaw, and a characteristically wrinkled forehead with quite broad ears. Unique among African hounds, it has a curled tail, with a white tip considered desirable.

There are a number of other distinctive features linked with this breed, although these may not be immediately apparent. The basenji is sometimes described as the barkless dog, because it is exceptionally quiet. This feature is valued by African huntsmen, because these hounds can approach close to their quarry without being detected, while in urban areas, it has also led to the rise in popularity of the basenji as a pet,

The distinctive, curled tail of the basenji, which is held close to the body, sets this breed apart from other hounds.

simply because it is unlikely to disturb near neighbours. Even so, the basenji is not dumb – when it does give voice, it has a highly distinctive yodelling call, expressing pleasure or excitement, while if disturbed, these hounds will growl.

In their homeland, basenjis are often fitted with bells when hunting, so that they can be followed in wooded areas more easily. Basenjis hunt by a combination of scent and sight, with their scenting ability being so acute that they can locate quarry up to 240ft (73m) away under ideal conditions. They hunt in small packs, although when kept together, basenjis can prove to be quite quarrelsome among themselves, in spite of their generally playful, affectionate natures. Around human settlements, basenjis will hunt and kill rodents, notably the long-toothed reed rat, while they will also drive larger quarry into nets and trail game.

These dogs first became known to European explorers in the late 19th century, with a pair being brought to England for the first time during 1895, sadly succumbing to distemper soon afterwards. It was not until 1936 that the basenji was reintroduced to England, with these particular hounds causing a sensation when they were exhibited at Cruft's for the first time in the following year. The breed became recognised under its present name, which had been given to it by Mrs Burn. It means 'bush thing' in the local Congolese dialect, reflecting some of the early names used for these hounds, which included African bush dog and Congo terrier, because of its predilection for hunting rodents.

Basenjis were rather susceptible to the diseases of the western dog world in the early days, and breeding proved to be more problematic than anticipated. This was because in common with wild canids and other pariahs, the basenji bitch only comes into season once a year, rather than twice as with almost all other domestic dogs. The breeding period typically extends from August to November.

Although these hounds are quite robust today and can be protected against the major killer diseases of the past such as distemper by vaccination, this still means that the availability of puppies through the year is strictly limited, being confined to the winter months. Another peculiarity is that basenjis often display a

Erect ears and a wrinkled forehead are other characteristics of this unusual breed, which has developed in relative isolation.

particular fondness for green vegetables, which can therefore be usefully included as part of their regular diet.

Young basenjis often have rather wayward natures, and can prove to be more destructive around the home than usual, particularly if they are left alone for any length of time. They mature into loyal, lively companions, and often make up for their relative lack of voice by using their feet to paw for attention, rather like some cats.

The distinctive, raised ridge of fur, which features in the name, Rhodesian ridgeback, can be clearly seen from this angle.

Basenjis are particularly clean hounds, spending long periods grooming themselves, rather like a cat. They are also far less affected by a noticeable 'doggy' odour than other breeds. Their short, sleek coat, with the distinctive white bib on the throat, is easy to keep in top condition with no more than the use of a hound glove. Perhaps not surprisingly in view of their origins, they dislike cold, damp weather and it may be advisable to select a suitable coat under these circumstances.

The other recognised breed of hound native to Africa is the Rhodesian ridgeback. Although developed in the southern part of the continent, it too may be related in part to those hounds occurring further north. The Rhodesian ridgeback is descended from crosses between European hounds, brought by the early settlers, and a native sighthound which was associated with the Hottentot (or khoi-khoin) tribespeople. They themselves had migrated south, bringing their distinctive hounds with them.

The Hottentot dog, as it was known, was characterised by a ridge of hair running down its back. Although now sadly extinct, this characteristic remains in the Rhodesian ridgeback – a feature shared only with the Thai ridgeback (see page 124), although it is unlikely that these contemporary breeds have any close relationship. The ridge of bristly hair grows in the reverse direction to the coat itself, so that it stands up. It is at its broadest across the withers, extending down the vertebral column and then tapering away close to the root of the tail.

Crossings between the European and African dogs were to result in a breed which had resistance to the illnesses prevalent in that part of Africa, plus speed, courage and good scenting skills. Modern development of the Rhodesian ridgeback was undertaken by the Reverend Helm during the 1870s. He introduced these hounds to Rhodesia (now known as Zimbabwe) from South Africa, where they had been kept by the Boer settlers in this region.

The Rhodesian ridgeback became highly valued by big game hunters of that era, in search of lions, to the extent that it also became known as the African lion hound for a time. The keen tracking skills of the breed, possibly reflecting a

ABOVE: Powerful and muscular, the Rhodesian ridgeback has been used to hunt lions.
BELOW: Dogs on average tend to be slightly larger in size than bitches in the case of this breed.

The ears of the Rhodesian ridgeback are set relatively high on the head, with the neck being well-muscled.

bloodhound ancestry, coupled with its stamina meant that riders on horseback could find lions without great difficulty. If ambushed or attacked by its quarry, the Rhodesian ridgeback was strong enough to defend itself.

The most famous examples of that early era were bred by Cornelius van Rooyen, who lived in the vicinity of Bulawayo, over a period of 35 years. After his death in 1922, moves were made to standardise the breed, and it was first recognised by the South African Kennel Club in 1922. Six years later, the first Rhodesian ridgebacks were imported to Britain and these hounds have since become popular in many countries.

A standard was established for them under the auspices of the American Kennel Club during 1959. In contrast to many hounds, the Rhodesian ridgeback is relatively easy to train. Its size and power make it a popular choice as a guard dog, while its affectionate nature makes the breed equally suitable as a household pet.

The muzzle in this breed is strong and deep, with the gums remaining taut against the jaws, rather than drooping.

CHAPTER 3
THE DEVELOPMENT OF HOUNDS IN BRITAIN, IRELAND AND FRANCE

One of the great difficulties in piecing together the development of dogs in general, quite apart from hounds, is the fact that in the past, archaeologists tended to be rather cavalier in their approach to canine remains found on sites of historical interest. There is no doubt that much potentially valuable information has been lost as a result.

In the early days of history however, it is clear that dogs served two main roles – as hunters and guardians. The first recorded evidence of the presence of dogs in Europe dates back over 9,000 years. One of these dogs has taken its name from an area known as Starr Carr, located in the English county of Yorkshire. There was already a clear divergence in appearance among domestic dogs by this time however, as revealed by a comparison of the Starr Carr dog with another of the same era unearthed from Senckenberg, which is close to Frankfurt am Main, Germany.

The bloodhound represents one of the oldest surviving European hound lineages.

While the Starr Carr dog has been likened to a contemporary terrier, the dog from Germany was of a larger size, with a pattern of dentition very similar in appearance to that of a contemporary domestic dog rather than a wolf.

Other subsequent finds from British sites indicate dogs which were probably not dissimilar to modern pariah dogs. There are no signs of specialisation in their skeletal structure. Even at this stage in history however, trade and travel was taking place on a perhaps surprisingly widespread scale. It could well have been that the dog skeletons unearthed on Windmill Hill, close to Avebury in Wiltshire, were derived from ancestral stock of Iberian origin. This area is known to have been settled in by the Beaker Folk who originated from this part of Europe, and subsequently settled in Britain, probably bringing their dogs with them.

Greyhounds in the past used to show much more diversity in appearance than the breed today.

The arrival of the Celts, around 400 BC, had a dramatic impact on the British landscape, thanks to their construction of hill forts, the remains of which can still be seen in many cases today. They also relied on dogs to help them guard their settlements. Large mastiffs were used for this purpose, with their fearless natures also being employed in hunting wild boar – a potentially dangerous quarry, although not especially fleet of foot. Mastiffs were also used in battle, gaining a particularly savage reputation in this role.

Julius Caesar recorded that his desire to obtain such dogs was one of the reasons which led him to invade Britain in 55 BC. The subsequent period of Roman settlement was to lead to dramatic changes in life style, which were reflected also by a rapid divergence in the types of dog being kept, as society became more settled.

It is likely that the number of dogs brought from abroad increased significantly during this period in history, as Roman staff were posted to the country from various parts of the empire. A detailed study of the remains of some 1,156 dogs unearthed from the Romano-British period surprisingly showed no evidence of ancestral greyhound-type stock, although this is probably not an accurate reflection of the canine population. This sample size would be tiny in any event, set against 450 years of Roman rule – equivalent to roughly 225 canine generations, assuming an average lifespan for dogs of seven years at that time.

Other evidence suggests that sighthounds were, however, represented in Britain by this stage. There are the Castor Ware drinking goblets and bowls, decorated with images of coursing greyhounds and quarry in the form of hares and deer, made in what is now the county of Northamptonshire. Further south-west, various Roman mosaics have been excavated on the pavements of the old town, called Corinium, and include images of two types of hound. One resembles a greyhound while the other is similar to the hounds known to exist across the English Channel in Gaul. Evidence of this type does not confirm that such hounds were in fact widely kept in Britain at that stage, but it is suggestive of this state of affairs, especially when combined with contemporary written accounts.

A list of Roman sporting breeds was compiled by Grattius, at some stage between 19 BC and 8 AD. Already, selective breeding was much in evidence, with Grattius claiming that crossing a Gaulish hound with an Umbrian bitch would yield offspring with superior hunting skills. It seems highly likely that the Romans would have been unable to resist the potential for mating such breeds from other parts of the Empire with those which they encountered in Britain, given the high reputation of the British hounds.

Almost certainly the breed known to the Romans as the *vertragus* was actually derived from the greyhound-type stock and had been introduced to Britain from Gaul. In fact, the name of these hounds was of Gallic origins. Grattius provides some valuable insight into their appearance, stating that they were characterised by yellow spots, having a coloured coat broken by white areas – not unlike the appearance of some contemporary hounds today.

He also commented on the great pace displayed by vertragi, highlighting the fact that they were less able to locate their quarry if it was hidden. This provides clear evidence that the vertragus was therefore a member of the sighthound group, using keen eyesight rather than scenting skills to locate its quarry. Vertragi were typically pitted against hares.

The identity of the relatively large prick-eared, hound-type dog featured in various mosaics unearthed in Britain is less clear. It may well have been the *segusius* however, as described by Arrian during the 2nd century AD. The segusius was clearly a much slower hound than the vertragus, rarely able to catch a hare. Instead, deer may have been its quarry, based on mosaic representations.

Standardisation within packs of hounds represents a more recent development in the evolution of this group of dogs.

The segusius reputedly had a melancholic voice, which is more indicative of a scenthound, and was probably long if not wire-coated.

Smaller in size, but more deadly in its tracking skills, was the other native type of British hound documented at that period. Known as the *agassaeus,* a detailed description of it was given by the Roman writer Oppian. He refers to its rounded shape, which may be suggestive of the roach back associated with greyhounds and whippets, as well as its skinny appearance.

The agassaeus possessed a shaggy coat however, more in keeping with many lurchers of today. It was also clearly a scenthound, credited with being able to pursue its quarry by relying on trails, both on the ground and in the air. Its teeth were also said to be formidable. Although showing distinctive hound-like attributes at this stage in history, it has been suggested that the agassaeus subsequently helped to found the terrier lineage, whose origins lie in Britain.

Various remains of dogs have been unearthed from the same period in history from sites in Ireland, including those of the fabled Irish hound, which may ultimately have given rise to the Irish wolfhound of today, a true giant of a dog standing 35in (90cm) high at the withers. The Irish hound itself was greatly respected for its strength, being able to dispatch not only wolves but also wild boar without human assistance. It had a justified reputation as a fearsome adversary. Such individuals were highly-prized. One particular Irish hound known as Allbé, owned by King Mesroda of Leinster, was so sought after by other kings in the country that huge sums were offered for him, but King Mesroda could not be persuaded to part with his hound at any price.

The origins of the Irish hound are not well-documented, but bearing in mind the size of the breed and its antiquity, it is perhaps even possible that it was native to Ireland. Irish hounds were likely to have resulted from cross-breeding of mastiff stock, which provided power and strength, with greyhound-type hounds introducing pace. They would have towered above the Irish wolfhound of today, measuring 4ft (1.2m) at the shoulder, with a huge head of 17in (43cm) in length. The majority were a light, sandy shade in terms of coloration.

Bloodhounds have provided inspiration for many artists and sculptors but this is actually a natural rock formation, called Dog Rock in Western Australia.

The wolfhound is the largest member of the hound grouping today, characterised by its gentle nature.

Such giants would certainly have been a target for the *procurator cynegii*, based for a period in Winchester during the Roman occupation of Britain. It was the responsibility of the holder of this office to obtain hounds to ship back to Rome. These were often pitted against savage quarry in the amphitheatres, having acquired apparently justified reputations for ferocity themselves. Some may have been used by emperors for hunting in the field as well.

Following the social breakdown which followed the collapse of the Roman Empire, dogs were abandoned. Contemporary accounts describe large packs roaming free, scavenging on whatever they could find to eat. Dogs became feared, partly because they might be infected by rabies, which could cause them to inflict a deadly bite on a person without warning, in an era long before vaccinations.

But the value of dogs was not entirely overlooked, and in areas where there was social stability, packs of hounds were kept for hunting purposes. The region of present-day France was an early centre for this pastime, with strict rules being enforced, firstly to permit hunting and secondly to prevent hounds from being killed by aggrieved persons without due cause.

The law decreed that only dogs known by their behaviour to be suffering from rabies could be killed, otherwise a fine, which increased quite dramatically from as little as three sous in 630 up to as much as 50 sous in the course of barely 150 years, was levied. Typical quarry in those days was not just wild boar and deer, but wolves as well, which were regarded as a social menace.

Hunting developed as a social pastime at this stage, and it appears to have become increasingly competitive. Although Mendelism and genetical theory lay a millennium into the future, selective breeding was practised, with those deemed to be the best hounds commanding large sums for stud purposes. Interestingly however, it was not the nobility at this stage who began to develop particular breeds, specialised for running down specific quarry, but monks who were alert to the commercial possibilities of this type of enterprise.

The ancestors of today's St Hubert hounds were developed during this era, being bred by the monks based at the Abbey of Saint Hubert, located in the Ardennes region of France. Saint Hubert himself was a huntsman, and the breed soon became widely kept, not just in France but much further afield. By donating six puppies every year to the King of France, which the monarch would then distribute to favoured nobles, the monks achieved great publicity and an enviable reputation for their breed.

The large, wide nostrils of the bloodhound assist its tracking skills, while the upper lips extend below the level of the lower jaw.

The St Hubert hound does not appear to have changed dramatically in appearance. It is better-known in the English speaking world as the bloodhound, because of its tracking skills. Tall, with broad ears and a furrowed brow, it displays great stamina, hunting primarily by scent rather than sight.

The growing significance of hunting in Europe can be seen from contemporary works of art, such as the hounds portrayed on the monument for Ferat Mac Batot, King of Gowrie, for a brief period during the 9th century. It is one of the earliest surviving portrayals of hounds in Britain, to be seen at St Vigeans in Angus. Another stone slab from this period shows a huntress, riding side-saddle, which confirms the growing social dimension to hunting. It was not considered fitting for ladies to ride astride.

There is evidence of skullduggery as well, in terms of seeking the best hounds, as recorded by the Scottish chronicler Hector Boece. He described how a group of Picts, visiting King Crathlint, were so impressed by the hounds which they saw that they persuaded some of the noblemen to give them some of the dogs. Still unsatisfied however, they then stole the king's best hound and subsequently murdered the king's Master of the Leash, who had been looking after it, when he challenged them.

It is quite difficult to gain any reliable insight into what was happening elsewhere in Britain. There is information about hounds contained within the Laws of Howell the Good, supposedly drawn up by the monarch at the start of the 10th century. The author described three types of hound present in Wales at that stage. There were buckhounds, regarded as the most valuable when trained, which were bay or dun in colour. Harriers were also mentioned in the context of their value, but they were apparently not present in Wales at that time. The other two groups of hounds described were scenthounds, known as *olrhëad* and the faster greyhound-type, called *milgi*.

Howell's code also contains details of how the hounds were used, being set against hinds (female deer) in the early months of the year, and then harts through the summer. The onset of winter marked the start of the boar hunting season.

Serious doubts have been expressed about the validity of this law code however, partly on the grounds of the hounds described in it. There is no doubt that the Irish hound was definitely present in Wales at that period in history, but there is no mention of it in this document, or indeed any hound which would have been pitted against wolves which were relatively common in the region at that time.

The problem posed by wolves in Wales was particularly acute, to the extent that Welsh rulers were compelled by their English masters to hunt wolves. Evidence in the form of wolf heads had to be provided by way of proof that the orders had been implemented. Hunting wolves with hounds required particular stamina, on the part of both the dogs and huntspeople, since wolves were usually able to match their domesticated cousins in terms of pace, and could exceed them in terms of cunning.

Other penalties involving hounds were also imposed on the Welsh. After defeating King Constantine at the Battle of Brunanburgh in 937, Athelstane demanded to be given hounds which were good trackers.

The development of hunting as a royal pastime in Britain began during the Dark Ages, with restrictions on the use of hounds for this purpose soon being savagely enforced. Alfred the Great (871–899) employed hounds to drive wild boar up towards waiting huntsmen armed with strong spears to kill them. Deer were caught in a rather similar fashion, being driven into nets in this case.

Hunting could be dangerous however, both for the hounds and the human participants. A royal disaster nearly occurred close to Ceoddri, involving King Edmund, who was Alfred's grandson. A stag being pursued by the pack leapt over a precipice followed by the hounds, and Edmund was only able to stop his mount right at the edge of the cliff.

King Canute (1016–1035) was responsible for outlawing the keeping of hounds by the majority of his subjects. Only the socially privileged could use hounds for hunting purposes. Any other dogs kept within the domain of the royal forests were deliberately handicapped, to restrict them from hunting effectively, by having either the tendons cut on their front legs or their claws removed.

This privilege was upheld even more ferociously during the Norman era. Hounds were highly prized, to the extent that those looking after them were charged with attempting to provide veterinary care should they fall ill or be injured. Bread rather than meat appears to have figured prominently in the diet of such dogs at that stage.

The growing obsession with using hounds for hunting purposes did not please everyone

however, particularly the Church. Priests and abbots were disbarred from keeping dogs, and the Emperor Charlemagne expressed his displeasure at members of the nobility turning up to worship with their favoured hounds. A ban resulted in a rather bizarre compromise whereby noblemen attended Mass outside the church, still in the company of their hounds, with the doors being left open so they were able to participate as normal in the service.

The priests responded by coming out to bless them, in a tradition carried through to the present day. The 'laying on of the pack' reflects a special link back to the hounds of that era.

The types of hound which had been prominent during the Dark Ages were still widely-kept through the medieval period, but they were joined in Europe by breeds from further afield. The Crusaders who travelled east to take part in the Holy Wars were accompanied by hounds as part of their retinues. They encountered others kept by their enemies, as well as their allies. King Louis XI of France (1461–83) returned with gazehounds, possibly of saluki stock, which he had used to hunt gazelle in the Middle East. As often happens when a new breed is introduced to another country today, this hound attracted mixed comments when it was first brought back to Europe. Enthusiasts of the gazehound claimed it was an exceedingly versatile dog, able to run at speed, with keen scenting abilities and considerable power. Its detractors viewed it as being lazy, noisy and unintelligent.

Short-legged breeds were developed in France, being called bassets thanks to the French word bas, *meaning* low *– a reflection of their stature close to the ground.*

Strength was not just useful for hunting; this attribute was still valued on the battlefield. There are various accounts of hounds seeking to protect wounded owners in this deadly environment. Gerald de Barri, writing in the 12th century, described how an Irish hound had fought bravely to save his master, and suffered seven wounds inflicted by lance and arrows in this vain attempt. Having survived this ordeal, the hound was treated for its injuries and survived, before ultimately being passed into the care of King Henry II (1154–89), who was a great dog-lover.

The long, thick tail of the bloodhound is very evident here, being carried erect, rather like a scimitar.

In another case, after Henry's army had been defeated in a battle in Wales, at a place called Coleshill, the body of a Welshman lay on the ground, guarded by his faithful hound. It refused to allow anyone near, driving off birds of prey, wolves and other dogs for over a week. So impressed were the English by the hound's devotion that its owner's body was finally buried with due ceremony rather than being left for the circling band of scavengers.

The loyalty of the hounds of that era was recorded in many other contemporary accounts, of which probably the best known is the story of Gelert, an Irish hound, although ironically, the origins of this particular tale are decidedly suspect. The dog in question was reputedly given by King John to his son-in-law, Llewelyn the Great, in 1205. They formed a strong bond, hunting together in the vicinity of Snowdon in Wales, according to the legend.

One day, Llewelyn set out hunting on his own, leaving Gelert to guard his infant son. When he returned, Llewelyn was distraught to see that the child's cot had been overturned and Gelert's jaws were stained with blood. He plunged his sword into the hound's heart, and as Gelert died, Llewelyn caught sight of his son, uninjured under a table in the room. Nearby lay the body of the wolf which Gelert had killed, defending the child. Horrified by what he had done, Llewelyn buried his beloved hound close to his hunting lodge. He marked the spot with a cairn of stones.

This tragic tale did not gain widespread attention until over 500 years later however, as it was made up by David Pritchard, when he became landlord of the Royal Goat Inn at the village of Beddgelert in Wales in 1793. This enterprising publican even buried a dog under a cairn to give credence to the story, with the assistance of the local parish clerk, but the fraud was finally unmasked when the remains were excavated. They came from a much smaller dog than an Irish hound.

Even so, the basis of the story was perhaps founded on fact. Similar accounts are given by ancient chroniclers of Wales, as far back as Cadog the Wise, who lived during the 5th century. The protective power of the hound which suffers an unjust death, is a recurring theme in medieval literature, and not just in Britain. A slightly different variation on this theme is reflected in the case of another Irish hound owned by a French nobleman, Aubri de Montdidier.

During 1371, de Montdidier was murdered by a close companion called Macaire, while they were out hunting together at Montargis. The hound returned and sought out its master's hidden grave, and remained in the locality for some time. It finally came back to Paris, seeking out the home of a friend of de Montdidier and led him to the grave. A chance meeting with Macaire at the royal court then resulted in the hound attempting to seize the murderer by the throat.

This occurred on several other occasions, whenever the hound saw Macaire. It became a matter of comment among other nobles, and the gossip reached the ears of the king, Charles VI (1380–1422). When the hound was brought before him in a room with Macaire and other noblemen, it again lunged ferociously at the murderer.

It was decided to settle the matter by Ordeal of Battle, which was a common means of resolving disputes at that time. The fateful encounter took place in Paris on the Ile de la Cité – there was no means of escape from here for either combatant. Macaire carried a wooden club, while a shelter was provided for the hound. Weighed down by leather armour and lacking the stamina of his opponent, Macaire dropped his guard sufficiently for the hound to spring at his throat. Finally, just before he died, Macaire admitted his guilt.

There are other accounts in history of hounds being able to identify their owners' murderers. Although this may seem rather fanciful, the scent of the person responsible will be present at the scene, which actually gives a rational basis to a dog's behaviour under these circumstances.

While some doubts have been expressed about the veracity of the Dog of Montargis tale, these accounts provide a valuable insight into the changing way in which dogs were perceived. The anthropomorphic aspects of such stories shine through very clearly – truth, loyalty, fidelity. Hounds were no longer viewed simply as animals, but rather as companions, encapsulating many of the virtues of the code of chivalry. The same attributes are highly-prized by owners of such dogs today.

In the medieval period, there is evidence of growing specialisation among the different types of dog which were then in existence. The Talbot hound, which is indelibly linked with the coat of arms of the Talbot family of Shrewsbury, Shropshire, was a scenthound, and an obvious ancestor of the bloodhounds. It was particularly valued for its tracking abilities, locating the whereabouts of those fleeing from the field of battle. In more peaceful times, such hounds were first used for pursuing injured deer with the trail of blood providing a strong scent for the dogs to follow, often over long distances.

One of the earliest published books on stag hunting, dating back to the 14th century, advised hunting with one of these scenthounds, not necessarily to track down the deer. The author emphasised just how much the hound can teach its owner about their quarry's behaviour by its actions.

The most famous manhunt of the medieval period, involving a Talbot hound, had the potential to change the whole course of history. Robert the Bruce (1306–1329), leading Scottish opposition to English rule, had actually reared the hound which ultimately was to pursue him into the hands of English knights. As the chase intensified, so Robert the Bruce divided his party into three, only to discover that the pursuing army was still on his trail.

Realising the danger, he then left his group in the company of his foster brother and drew off his English foes, who were being assisted by Bruce's captured Talbot hound. The English commander, John of Lorn, sensing a moment of opportunity, sent the hound ahead with five of his best soldiers, to kill or capture Robert the Bruce. A vicious encounter followed, which left all the pursuers dead, while Bruce and his foster brother were unharmed. There are those who believe that Bruce's Talbot hound may well have assisted his former master to dispatch his foes at this point. They then escaped any further risk of pursuit by wading down a stream to safety.

The Talbot hound was known under various other names, including sleuth hound, limehound and liam. Its tracking skills were often employed in pursuing criminals, such as cattle-rustlers, especially in the border region between England and Scotland. Such hounds represented a significant advance in the battle for law and order, with the skills of this group of dogs having been employed by people for this purpose now for almost a thousand years.

What had begun and certainly continued for a period as an important means of obtaining food, soon developed into a social pastime as well. The scale of hunting in Britain was such that there were 800 parks, 69 royal forests and 13 chases in England alone, during the reign of William the Conqueror (1066–1087).

He ordered strict controls on those keeping dogs within these areas, to prevent unauthorised hunting. Aside from mutilations of greyhounds to prevent them pursuing game, dog gauges were also introduced for the first time. These devices were used to determine whether a dog was large enough to be a threat to the game, although the height of the gauge was not actually standardised.

Greyhounds have been evolved for their pace, rather than their stamina. Restrictions on ownership to prevent poaching were common.

Hunting so dominated the lives of kings during the medieval period that they even conducted government business in forest clearings. Meanwhile, the penalties that could be imposed for poaching had become increasingly severe – they included blinding, castration and amputation of the hands and feet. Even so, most supposed transgressions were punished by fines, which came to be viewed almost as taxes because of the difficulties of defending such allegations. Poor people with greyhounds were compelled to attend the Forest Courts in any event, which were held every three years, to determine whether their hounds might have been running amok at any stage in the forest.

Aside from the nobility, hunting rights were also sometimes extended to members of the clergy, who could maintain hounds for use in the royal forests. Many clerics were keen hunters, having time to pursue their interests in the field. William de Clowne, Abbot of St Mary's in Leicestershire became the accepted authority on hare hunting, providing advice both to Henry III (1216–72) and his son Prince Edward on this topic. William's request that he should be permitted to organise a regular sale for hounds and other dogs, in order to maintain the quality of his kennels, was, perhaps not surprisingly, granted. The hunting rights of other clerics were usually more restricted. Those resident at Chertsey Abbey, for example, could only hunt foxes, hares and pheasants with their hounds.

The favours bestowed on such dogs by their owners was often the subject of adverse comment and criticism. Pope Innocent received a formal complaint about the Archdeacon of Richmond, because of his large hunting entourage, particularly his hounds, which had to be fed on bread, consuming supplies set aside for the monks of Bridlington. The Pope responded by condemning such visits.

One of the most serious acts of the medieval period – the slaying of Thomas à Becket – can be linked with hounds. Becket himself was a keen huntsman and it was the theft of his hounds which led him to take the fatal decision to excommunicate his enemies. This decision was ultimately to lead to Becket's murder in 1170 within Canterbury Cathedral in Kent.

Hunts of the medieval period could be protracted affairs, with the result that the entourage would not be able to return to their point of departure at the end of the day. In some cases, they may have been able to journey on to another noble's castle, or alternatively they could seek accommodation at a monastery which was probably another reason why clerics were encouraged to become active participants in hunting.

Convents were also expected to play host to hunting parties, although at such establishments, the keeping of hounds was actively discouraged and frequently outlawed by the ecclesiastical authorities. The presence of hounds in cloisters meant that services could be disturbed by their barking, while alms that supposedly should have been used for the poor and needy were spent on feeding the dogs, according to contemporary accounts. Yet such complaints were not an apparent cause for concern at monasteries, whose occupants could hunt!

A detailed account of the hounds used for hunting and the way in which they were kept as the medieval period drew to a close is provided by Edward, the 2nd Duke of York, writing at the start of the 15th century. He describes the kennel building provided for his own hounds, made of timber and measuring 60ft (18m) in length and 25ft (7.6m) in breadth. The hounds slept on straw bedding, with a central drain. There was even a fire with a chimney, so that the hounds could dry off in a warm environment. The kennel boy would sleep in the storey above the hounds, watching them closely for signs of rabies, which was apparently not uncommon at that time, and greatly feared, since it could decimate a pack.

Fresh air was an important feature of the kennel's design with doors constantly being left open for this reason, leading into an exercise paddock. This grassy area was carefully sited, to ensure that it was sunny here throughout the day, as far as possible.

Security was also important, with the kennel area being protected by a barricade of sharp wooden spikes. Entry to the kennel area was through a portcullis-style door, guarded by a mastiff. The kennel boy would spend all his time looking after the hounds. He was even expected to spin leashes to allow them to be coupled when taken out of the kennels.

The greyhound, in its diverse forms, was still the most popular hunting breed in Britain at that stage, although in mainland Europe, according to Gaston III de Foix et de Béarn, a contemporary and relative of Edward, and author of *Le Livre de Chasse*, there were Brittany and Gascon hounds, St Hubert hounds and even small greyhounds well-represented in kennels.

The griffon fauve de Bretagne. Its origins in France date back as far as the Middle Ages.

By the late 14th century, there was growing concern expressed by the nobility that their beloved greyhounds were being kept by others, including servants – a trend strongly disapproved of by Edward. He relates how his greyhounds were well-trained even in church, and accompanied him throughout the day, feeding from table scraps and ranging freely around his home.

Many different breeds of French hound have been developed, showing regional variations in many cases.

It is clear from contemporary descriptions that the term 'greyhound' related to a number of different types of hound at that stage. It was very much a general term. Basically, such dogs had an athletic build, enabling them to run at speed, in contrast to the more plodding gait of the Talbot hound and its congenitors.

York refers to the Irish hound, and the evolving Scottish deerhound bred from Irish stock. At the other extreme is the small, slender Italian greyhound, which could be pitted against hares. There were both rough and smooth-coated greyhounds. York himself recommends greyhounds of medium size, since they could be used against any type of quarry which might be sprung.

The hunt also relied on scenthounds, which were used to locate and flush game in the first instance. Greyhounds were trained so that as well as pursuing game, they could also drive it towards waiting hunters. The versatility of the greyhound when hunting, meaning that it would pursue any quarry from a hare to deer or wolves, ensured that those keeping greyhounds were almost automatically assumed to be hunting with them.

Relatively little is recorded about the coloration of such hounds, although white appears to have been popular. Gaston Phoebus favoured those which were fallow-red in appearance. His description of the most suitable type of greyhound is not dissimilar to that of the breed today. He highlights a long head, small ears, an arched neck, a broad chest, powerful shoulders, straight legs coupled with large claws and cat-shaped feet as desirable characteristics.

While greyhounds were considered to be social by nature, the Talbot hound enjoyed a special relationship with its master. It had a particular role in tracking down game at the start of the hunt, being known as a 'liam' after the long leash on which it ranged in search of quarry. The liam measured at least 21ft (6.3m) long, and was made of tough, well tawed horse hide. More decorative liams could be worn when the hound was not working. They were made of expensive materials such as velvet and silk, with the collar being decorated with pearls.

Talbots were relatively expensive dogs to keep, being fed again mainly on bread. Wheat, oats and bran were used in bread provided as food in the kennels. Hounds were given the entrails of their quarry to eat however, after a successful kill.

While at the start of the medieval era, hunting was largely an informal pastime, it had evolved into a more complex, structured activity as that period of history drew to a close. Deer hunting in particular developed on an artificial basis, often being carried out within a confined area so that the quarry had no chance of escape from the hounds.

Known as the *battue*, this means of hunting meant that the speed of the hounds was less significant, as they could not be ultimately outpaced.

There were significant changes taking place however, that would impact on the development of the hounds themselves and lead in due course to the evolution of new types of hound. Hare hunting continued to build up a strong following, partly because the hare proved to be a fast, agile adversary and yet posed no danger to either hounds or huntsmen. It appealed to those seeking less formality when hunting – generally the less wealthy sectors of society.

The hunting of wolves and wild boar was in decline by the late medieval period, as the numbers of these animals had already fallen significantly in various parts of Europe. Partly for this reason therefore, emphasis switched towards hunting the fox, which may have been increasing in numbers at this stage, as wolves gradually became eliminated from many areas.

In mainland Europe, the fox was regarded as little more than a pest, to be eliminated as simply as possible. Gaston Phoebus gave a range of options to increase the likelihood of catching foxes in France, which included smoking them out of their underground earths and blocking up the entrances to prevent a fox seeking sanctuary there.

This was not apparently in accord with hunting practices in Britain however, where the fox was deemed a worthy opponent and respected accordingly. Fox hunting began in earnest during the reign of King John (1199–1216). There are references to both running hounds and foxhounds in contemporary accounts, although it was not until much later (see page 60) that the foxhound was developed as a distinctive breed. Greyhounds also featured in packs kept for fox hunting purposes, in spite of their reputation for being disinterested in pursuing foxes.

The cost of fox hunting was considerable however, requiring a relatively large entourage, although this activity took place with the followers on foot, rather than mounted. There could be thirty or more hounds in a pack, and they in turn needed to be supervised by as many as a dozen people.

One of the appeals of fox hunting was that it could be fitted into the autumn through to spring period when other types of hunting were not generally pursued. Such was the aristocratic obsession with hunting at that stage that the costs incurred were therefore a price almost invariably considered to be worth paying.

The whippet has evolved into a smaller breed than the greyhound, although standardisation is a relatively recent phenomenon in the canine world, having come to the fore as the result of the development of show standards in the late 1800s.

Italian greyhound. This breed arose as the result of a trend towards miniaturisation of the greyhound itself, to create a lap dog which became popular around the royal courts of Europe. Unfortunately, scaling down in this way and soundness are not always compatible.

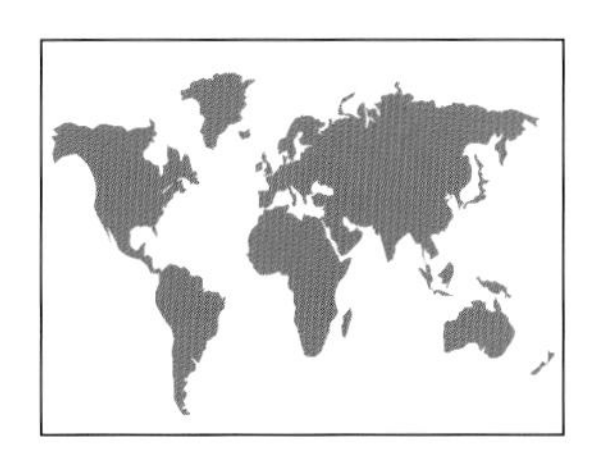

Chapter 4
Through to the Modern Era

As in so many other walks of life, the Renaissance led to a reassessment of the relationship between dogs and people. During the medieval period, dogs had inspired mixed emotions. They were highly regarded in many cases, as reflected by the tombs in churches portraying greyhounds in the company of their noble owners, and yet the term 'hound' was also considered to be a term of particularly unpleasant abuse. When Piers Gaveston, confidant of King Edward III (1327–77), described the Earl of Warwick as 'The black hound of Arden', the insult was ultimately to cost Gaveston his life. He was executed later on Warwick's orders for this insult.

The Renaissance led to a more rational view of the importance of hounds and other dogs in society, and with the growth of interest in scientific matters, there was an apparently insatiable quest for knowledge about them.

The advent of printing meant that works such as *La Vénérie* (The Science of Hunting), written by the Frenchman Jacques du Fouilloux could become widely read, with editions being published in other languages as well. Past classics, which previously had only a very restricted readership, now reached a much wider audience. Foremost among these was the treatise on animal diseases by a Franciscan monk called Bartholomew Glanville. By 1500, it was circulating in no less than seventeen different languages.

There was much more interest in the successful management of dogs, as witnessed by the popularity of George Tuberville's book entitled *The Selection, Hygiene and Illnesses of the Dog*, published in 1590. Specialist works were also available such as *Livre des Chiens pour la Chasse*, (Book of Hunting Dogs) which was published in 1492 on the orders of Charles VIII by Guillaume Tardif, based in Navarre, France.

During the Renaissance era, the greyhound grouping began to become clarified, as three recognisable types emerged. There were those which resembled the greyhound of today, as well as a much smaller variant, apparently not dissimilar in appearance to the Italian greyhound. The third group comprised the largest individuals, and apparently evolved in Brittany.

Hunting with greyhounds remained highly popular among the nobility in both Britain and France. Yet subtle changes had begun at this stage, with greyhounds being crossed with what were described as gazelle hounds, first brought back from the Middle East by the Crusaders, in order to improve their pace. This in turn led to them being used for coursing. This was a very different type of hunting, compared with the bear and boar hunting which greyhounds had participated in previously.

Coursing entailed two greyhounds being kept on leashes, and released to pursue a hare which had been given a start of some 35yd (32m) or so. It was not the first greyhound to catch the hare which was adjudged winner of the contest. Rather, the greyhound that caused the hare to pause, turn and race off in another direction was considered the more talented courser.

Coursing itself became popular with the nobility of various other European countries, including France, where it led to a dramatic

St Hubert hound and basset hound. The ancestral role played by the bloodhound in the development of the basset is clearly visible, reflecting the close links between the hounds of Britain and France.

decline in the hare population during the late 1600s, following the importation of about 20,000 greyhounds. Spain too enthusiastically embraced coursing, although the native greyhound breed, known today as the Galgo Español, is slower than its English relative.

Yet it was not just English hounds that had an impact on the broader European scene. The grand chien blanc du roi was a hound of French origin, which was to have a major impact on the distinctive breeds of pack hound which have since evolved in many parts of Europe.

It is said that this lineage was evolved from a stud dog which lived in Poitou, called Souillard. These hounds were large in size and characterised by their pure white coloration. Mary, Queen of Scots, sent one of her St Hubert hounds, a white individual called Baraud, to France and he apparently made a notable contribution to the evolving bloodline. These were hounds famed not just for their coloration, but also for their beauty.

There was no lessening of interest in hunting with hounds during the Renaissance period. Indeed, when Louis XIII (1610–43) died, he had over 90 people employed exclusively to assist with this pastime. Training was onerous and lengthy, with an apprenticeship lasting three years. During the final year, the apprentice worked each day with a specific bloodhound, becoming proficient in understanding their quarry.

Costs continued to soar under Louis XIV (1643–1715), with the great kennels being constructed in 1685 on what is now the site of the Versailles Prefecture. All the king's packs of hounds could then be kept on this single site. The list reveals the increasing specialisation that was taking place, as hounds were evolved increasingly to pursue particular quarry.

Hares were hunted using a special pack of hounds brought from Champagne, while strong, powerful Anglo-French hounds were kept to pursue wild boar and other large game. Scottish deerhounds were also resident at these kennels, being pitted against roe deer. Wolves however, which remained more numerous in France than in Britain, were hunted by white Pyrenean mountain dogs, which are of mastiff stock, rather than being allied with hound breeds.

Word about the magnificent collection of hounds kept not just by Louis XIV, but also by his son the Dauphin and leading nobles such as the Duke de Vendôme spread through Europe and further afield, even to the King of Siam, in whose Asiatic kingdom the breed of hound now described as the Thai ridgeback (see page 124) had evolved.

The royal kennels underwent a significant change however, towards the end of the reign of Louis XIV. As he became older, so the king was no longer able to ride to hounds, and was forced to follow the outcome on wheels. This decline in his health spelt the end of the white hound lineage, simply because they were too fast to be followed in this fashion. As a result, these hounds were crossed with slower Normandy hounds, starting around 1700. The origins of the Normandy hound itself is unclear, but it seems likely that they were related in part to the St Hubert, being tricoloured in appearance. They stood between 26 and 30in (65 and 76cm) tall and had acquired a reputation as good trackers.

When Louis XV (1715–1774) succeeded to the throne, he sought to recreate the fabled white hounds, and in order to do so, he sought cross-bred hounds from Britain. This strongly suggests that some white hounds must have been sent to England at an earlier stage in history, and may presumably still have existed in a relatively pure state.

The tongue of the bloodhound is important in allowing these hounds to maintain their body temperature. Panting causes evaporation of saliva and dissipates heat from the body.

Even so, there was a fundamental difference in the way that the white hound ran, compared with British hounds. It was a sighthound noted for its pace, able to overcome the fittest stags in barely 45 minutes, whereas a much slower hunt was preferred in Britain, with hounds tracking predominantly by scent.

The obsession with hunting changed the entire British landscape, with huge areas given over to deer parks and oak trees which provided the essential timber to provide barriers around the perimeter of these parks. This dependence on oak served the country well however, in providing strong timber to construct ships which engaged the Spanish Armada in 1588 and set out on the voyage of discovery around the globe. The obsession with hounds which had become so prevalent in Britain ultimately brought a lasting national benefit.

The advent of the Tudor dynasty marked the end of the era of the deer park however, with Henry VIII issuing an edict in 1536 that all owners of such parks had to keep mares in them, for breeding purposes, so as to increase the country's horse population.

A further curb on the canine population resulted from Henry's order that no dogs of any kind – including hounds – should be kept at court, apart from his own! Hunting effectively became more mechanised, with game being shot by crossbows or caught in nets, although greyhounds were still often used to drive the game towards the marksmen. Unfortunately, this also put the hounds in the line of fire, and they could themselves be killed as a consequence.

Deer coursing did take place on occasions however, and proved to be a much safer option for the hounds. The deer were chased up the course, with stragglers being pulled down, while the stronger individuals were able to jump the large ditch at the end, escaping from their pursuers.

The first attempt to classify the various types of hounds and other dogs then in existence was made by Dr John Caius. He was a divinity graduate of what was then Gonville College Cambridge (now Gonville and Caius), and subsequently obtained a medical degree from Padua, becoming court physician to Edward VI, then Mary and finally Queen Elizabeth I.

Caius was asked by Conrad Gesner, a leading Swiss naturalist of the period, for information on the various types of dog extant in Britain during the sixteenth century. Caius's reply, written in Latin, was published under the title *De canibus Britannicis*, and provides a unique insight into the evolution of domestic dogs, including the different varieties of hound that were being kept at that stage.

Unfortunately, the resulting English translation which appeared in 1576 did not clarify Caius's ideas on the classification of the different varieties. He did recognise hounds, notably bloodhounds and harriers, as a sub-group within the thoroughbred or 'generous' category. Other types of hound were featured on his listing as hunting dogs. These included greyhounds, gazehounds, tumblers and limers. Almost certainly, this separation occurred because these latter breeds actually displayed much greater variability in appearance at that time, compared with those in the thoroughbred grouping.

Greyhounds were kept primarily for hunting deer in this period, although they were also used to hunt foxes on occasions. In the north of the country, gazehounds were especially popular for tackling both foxes and hares.

There are those who question Caius's knowledge of the breeds then in existence, because the limer was apparently identical to the bloodhound, which of course was in his thoroughbred rather than hunting category. Such dogs were typically used to hunt down wounded quarry. Caius mistakenly claims that they could run quickly, whereas in fact such hounds possessed more stamina than pace.

His description of 'tumbler' refers to a dwarf form of greyhound, possibly related to the Italian breed, which was used for hunting rabbits. Lurchers also appear to have been in existence by this era, hunting silently after dark. This was an essential attribute in a poacher's hound, if the local gamekeeper was not to be alerted to his presence.

Bloodhounds were also trained to work after dark, particularly in the Borders district, between England and Scotland. They were even reportedly kept in darkened kennels, as this was thought to

The black saddle on the bloodhound's back between its legs is a feature seen in many breeds descended from this ancient lineage.

improve their night-time vision, according to Caius. One of the most highly valued attributes of the bloodhound was the way in which it could pursue an individual by scent, without being deterred by other people in a crowded area. The only way to throw one of these hounds off the trail was to plunge into water, wading along the river or stream before continuing on land. Travelling a short distance in this way would only bring temporary respite for the fugitive.

Capture of a person thanks to a bloodhound's scenting skill was seen as tantamount to a verdict of guilt, while those obstructing such hounds were likely to be viewed as accessories to the crime.

Bloodhounds in the Borders region between England and Scotland were described by Caius as either red (presumably a dark shade of fawn) or black, with their coats broken by coloured spots. This lineage remained quite common in this area right up until the 1700s, while other bloodhounds were despatched overseas (see page 128) to the New World and elsewhere, where their tracking skills were in great demand. Contemporary accounts indicate that these hounds were then much fiercer in temperament than their descendants of today. They would sometimes even eat an unfortunate victim.

Although bloodhounds were usually hunted on foot, they were sometimes used with pursuing riders, so they could keep the huntsmen on the track of their quarry if it disappeared from view. Such bloodhounds were apparently less common however, and often needed special training for this task.

The links between English and French hounds were strengthened by the accession of James I (1603–1625). He brought French hounds and accompanying experts to advise his courtiers, establishing a faster type of pursuit than had previously been favoured in England. Newmarket became the social centre for hunting, although there were various impositions placed on subjects elsewhere in the country, to ensure that the king and his associates could hunt in relative safety. In Hertfordshire for example, the farmers in the county were prohibited from allowing their pigs to wander freely, because they would root up the ground, creating a depression that could cause a horse to trip and unseat its rider.

Otter hunting underwent a revival in popularity at this stage with millers being compelled to block off waterways to assist the hunt. James appointed Henry Mynours as Master of the Otterhounds, with powers to take dogs for this purpose. There was no particular type of dog favoured for the task of otter hunting. Mynours' powers specifically covered hounds, beagles, spaniels and even mongrels, so that packs for this purpose were clearly variable in appearance.

The king and his entourage placed further demands on the people, to the extent that complaints were made, perhaps none more dramatically than when Jasper, a hound which was particularly favoured by James, disappeared overnight. The hound mysteriously turned up on the following day, with a note advising the king that all the provisions had been used up, thanks to the demands of his people. The note's writer asked Jasper to convey this information to the king, since James heard him every day, but did not hear his subjects. While this would have been seen as treacherous under certain circumstances, the king perhaps wisely decided to make light of the matter and treated it as a joke.

Part of the reason for the resentment displayed towards James compared with his immediate predecessors is that he took over the countryside when hunting, rather than confining his activities to the deer parks owned by his nobles. The faster style of hunting also reinforced the feelings of those over whose land James and his entourage rode.

A pack typically numbering between twenty and thirty hounds would be set on the trail of some deer, which were the favoured royal quarry. They were accompanied by riders galloping on horseback, which invariably meant that any barriers such as fences in their path were likely to be smashed, with no reparations being made for the resulting damage.

The style of hunting developed by King James was ultimately to lead to the breeding of hounds specifically for the chase. Standardisation was on the way, creating breeds such as the foxhound and its American relative, which are still kept

A lemon and white basset hound puppy. Tricolours are also common in this breed.

The trend towards standardisation in pack hounds meant that hunting became a more organised pursuit, and led directly to the development of the foxhound.

essentially as hunting dogs rather than household pets.

In the interim however, such was the disdain with which James was viewed by many of his subjects that they decided to take matters into their own hands. There was an upsurge in the poaching of the king's deer, to the extent that James was forced to issue a proclamation on this matter in 1609. He did not favour the shooting of deer with either longbows or crossbows, partly because he did not consider this to be sport. His views in this respect hardened following the death of one of his favourite hounds called Jewel, which met an untimely end when he was accidentally shot by the queen, Anne of Denmark in 1613.

James' reign also marked the start of opposition to hunting on moral grounds. The Puritans, whose influence was to grow considerably through the reign of his successor Charles I (1625–1649), before taking control of the country as a result of the Civil War, held hunting to be an ungodly pursuit. They cited biblical references in support of their view, even in the king's presence on one notable occasion.

Nevertheless, there were leading figures among the Puritans who had a clear affiliation with hounds, such as Oliver Cromwell's uncle, and indeed Cromwell himself. Their family was among those forced to present King Charles I with fast hounds. Deep ill-feeling spread through the country in 1628 after Lord Compton, who held the office of Master of His Majesty's Leash, was empowered to take greyhounds and other dogs to add to Charles's packs.

The situation was made even worse by Charles's desire to regain control over royal forests which had passed to the ownership of others, often centuries earlier. This policy was imposed as a means of raising further revenue for the king, rather than extending his own personal hunting opportunities. Nevertheless, those owning hounds were no longer able to hunt within these areas and faced having their dogs seized, destroyed or crippled.

By this stage, there were recognisable differences between hounds bred in different parts of the country. The fastest, lightest hounds in England were to be found in the north of the country, in counties such as Northumberland and Cumbria. On the western side, extending from Cheshire and Lancashire southwards, the hounds were larger in size, but had much slower pace. Those of middle England were of intermediate size and pace, with what subsequently became known as the pocket beagle, because of its small size, also being widely kept in this area. A contemporary description refers to these hounds as being suitable to be carried in a man's glove.

When the level of discontent with the monarch finally led to the outbreak of Civil War, hunting came to the aid of the Royalists. Their cavalry forces were comprised of highly skilled horsemen, and in this respect they proved to be vastly superior to their Parliamentarian opponents, however, it was not enough to rebuff the Parliamentarians.

Perhaps surprisingly, when Cromwell formed the Protectorate, the use of hounds for hunting purposes continued. No longer were there to be deer hunts, if only because the deer population had been largely massacred during the popular unrest of the Civil War years. Instead, attention switched to smaller quarry, notably hares, with Cromwell himself having a greyhound which hunted regularly. It was rather ironically called Coffin-nail.

Fox hunting, although not held in high regard at this stage, started to grow in popularity. The surviving descendants of the royal buckhounds were pitted against foxes, probably on grounds of political and practical expediency.

After the Restoration in 1660, Charles II attempted to restock the deer parks, enabling hunting to begin again, but it proved impossible to obtain the required stags, even from mainland Europe. Life had changed irrevocably. The king interested himself in horse racing at Newmarket, and presided over dog racing, most notably the Hampton Court Olympic, which was held near the palace, and drew thousands of spectators. The races themselves were accompanied by heavy betting on the participants. Perhaps surprisingly however, it was not until the middle of the 19th century that dog racing became established as a sport, complete with carefully drawn rules.

Charles himself was a genuine dog-lover, as reflected by the breeds of toy spaniel which bear his name. There was a corresponding increase in the dogs represented at Court, with pocket beagles being regarded as dual-purpose hounds. They could hunt well, while at the same time, they also served as ladies' companions. Their subsequent demise may be traced perhaps to a lack of soundness, resulting from the scaling down of size – a common problem associated with other breeds, ranging from poodles to Yorkshire terriers.

Another miniature variety of hound which has a modern counterpart is the Italian greyhound. These dogs were perceived, rather critically in some quarters, as being only suitable as companions for elderly ladies. Their lack of protective instincts, as shown by their refusal to bark loudly at the approach of strangers, was condemned. They also gained a reputation for being delicate, often having to be wrapped in clothes to keep them warm during the winter.

Even so, Italian greyhounds were crossed with established British greyhound stock, contributing an elegance which had been lost in some cases as the result of crossings taking place with bulldogs. At that stage in history bulldogs were a much longer-legged, athletic type of dog than the bulldog of today.

The refinement and development of hounds and other sporting dogs began in earnest during the 18th century, pioneered by a variety of enthusiasts. Coursing was especially popular during this era, and two men played a vital role in developing the greyhound during this period. Lord Orford (1730–91) resided primarily in Norfolk and here he established the Swaffham Coursing Society. As the grandson of Robert Walpole, Orford had inherited the former Prime Minister's love of hunting.

The appeal of hounds simply as companions was begun by the Italian greyhound. Such dogs soon became popular in royal circles across Europe.

Walpole had hunted regularly across Richmond Park with his own pack of beagles, and was noted for opening correspondence from his gamekeeper before any other letters.

Orford maintained kennels of about 100 greyhounds and was a genuine devotee of these hounds. His interest spanned the social spectrum, so that he was able to converse equally with poachers as much as other peers, seeking views as to how the emerging breed could be developed. Orford believed that greater stamina had to be introduced to these hounds, as well as speed, in order to improve their coursing abilities.

Many were unconvinced about the wisdom of crossing bulldogs with greyhounds, but Orford persevered regardless. After seven generations, it was universally agreed that this breeding programme had produced the best greyhounds which had yet been bred. They excelled not only in terms of characteristics associated with these hounds, such as a thin coat and small ears, but also in pace and determination.

The use of the Italian greyhound served to restore the breed's athletic appearance but there were risks attached to this type of breeding programme, simply because the attributes of the greyhound could be lost. Orford himself encountered this problem when he crossed these sighthounds with bloodhounds which of course hunt by scent. The resulting progeny displayed a greater tendency to follow their noses rather than their eyes.

Orford's obsession with hounds nearly proved fatal when he decided to use four red deer stags to pull his phaeton (carriage) rather than horses. He used this odd arrangement for a time with great success, and the deer carriage became a noted sight in the locality, often heading to the Ram Inn at Newmarket.

Unfortunately however, on one occasion, a pack of hounds picked up the scent of the deer and set off in pursuit of them. The stags became virtually uncontrollable and the phaeton, with

The local terrain had a significant impact on the development of many hound breeds, as did the style of hunting. Basset hounds lack the pace of longer-legged breeds, and are accompanied on foot rather than on horseback.

Lord Orford attempting to remain in control, lurched off at great speed. Luckily, Orford was just able to steer his stags into the yard adjoining the inn, where with the help of stable boys and others, they were hurried into a barn. The gate was closed just as the pursuing hounds caught up with this unlikely ensemble.

Ultimately, it was coursing which killed Orford. After the death of his mistress, Orford suffered a mental breakdown, which meant that he should have been under supervision. Slipping out through an open window however, he rode off to a coursing match where his best bitch of that period, called Czarina was involved. Orford rode through the crowd, following the greyhounds, and sustained a fatal fall just as his bitch won the contest.

There was a certain irony attached to this, since as a result of his endeavours, coursing had become accepted as a social pastime which women could both attend and in whose management they could assist. The Swaffham Society was graced by lady patronesses, and this in turn helped to ensure that when dog showing developed at a later stage, women were free to participate in this activity, whereas they were excluded from many other aspects of Victorian life.

Following Orford's death, his greyhounds, including Czarina, were sold. Luckily, she and a number of the other leading examples were purchased by an equally enthusiastic breeder called Colonel Thomas Thornton, at what was considered to be a bargain price.

When Thornton took his new acquisitions from the flat countryside of Norfolk up to the Yorkshire Dales however, there were those who doubted the wisdom of his purchases. While the hares were able to stop and turn easily on the steep hillsides in this part of the country, Orford's greyhounds often lost their footing and rolled down the slopes. He had bred them for pace rather than agility.

This part of England had been one of the last strongholds of the wolf, which had finally been exterminated towards the end of the 15th century. Thornton's own strain of greyhounds was descended from the wolfhounds which had brought about their demise. They therefore had an innate ability to hunt effectively on these hills, honed over generations. They differed significantly in appearance from the soft, short-coated Norfolk greyhounds, with their long coats reflecting their wolfhound ancestry.

By crossing these two different lineages, Thornton's faith was justified – out of one particular litter, three unrivalled greyhounds emerged. Two of these, called Major and Sylvia, ultimately retired undefeated, while the third, christened Snowball, had a special tomb erected in his honour on his demise, in the guise of a Grecian urn and pedestal. This began a fashion which has developed and continued through to the present day.

Unfortunately, Thornton's mental health deteriorated, as had Orford's, and he suffered greatly from delusions of self-grandeur. His hunting entourage became vast and unsustainable, in spite of his gambling successes which helped to support his affluent lifestyle. Financial disaster followed, forcing Thornton to sell up in 1819 and move to France where he died in penury.

Gambling had become an integral part of coursing by this time, much as in due course, greyhound racing was to be supported by betting on the outcome of the event. The actual hunting of hares also changed. It had been a leisurely event where the intention was not to kill the hare, but to enjoy the thrill of the chase. It was regarded as a flaw for packs of harriers to overwhelm their quarry, up until the 18th century when this view started to change.

Hare hunting took place when the harvest was over, leaving the hares more exposed, but the hunt itself faced the problem of a shortage of

The whippet is one of the fastest of all hounds, and is also very agile when running.

Dog racing is a popular sport today, originating as a result of the development of hounds with greater pace during the 18th century.

daylight at this stage. The hounds started at dawn, tracking down the hare to where it was hidden, and then they were called off, allowing the hare to race away. The chase began in earnest at this stage, although there were a growing number of huntsmen who found the build-up to the chase itself protracted in the extreme, compared with fox hunting which was increasing rapidly in popularity during the second half of the 18th century.

The significant changes which then occurred had far-reaching consequences for the hounds. Most existing packs of harriers at that stage were based on the Southern hound, which was of ancient stock and probably an offshoot of the lineage that ultimately led to today's bloodhound. They were dedicated scenthounds, rather lacking in pace, but large in stature, measuring approximately 22in (55cm) tall.

At this stage, as with greyhounds and other hounds, the description of 'harrier' was generic, rather than being indicative of a particularly recognisable type of dog. In Manchester for example, there were two prominent packs of harriers, one derived from Southern hound stock, while the other consisted of beagles.

As in the case of greyhounds, there were recognised local variants, such as Cotswold beagles, famed for their pace, and the North Country beagles which ultimately evolved into the contemporary harrier. The Southern hound packs were the first to suffer from the changes in hare hunting practice. They died out towards the end of the 18th century, with their lack of pace proving fatal in the face of competition from the more versatile and athletic beagle.

Nor was the Southern hound to be the only casualty in this era, when across the English Channel, the French Revolution broke out in August 1789. The egalitarian nature of this uprising spelt the demise of many of the packs of hounds that had been kept for hunting purposes at *châteaux* throughout the country. There had been considerable specialisation, which had arisen in part because of *venery*, meaning the art and science of hunting.

The scientific aspect was reflected in the development of hounds to pursue particular types of game, with the origins of most French hounds thought to extend back to the original St Hubert hound. Even so, there were considerable differences in appearance in the case of these ancestral hounds, to the extent that there was no consistent type. Almost certainly, crossings involving hounds from other parts of Europe, including Britain, also occurred and the great white hound or grand chien blanc de roi played a significant part as well.

It is difficult to state with certainty the number of types of hound which were lost as a result of the French Revolution, particularly as some *châteaux* simply favoured a specific colour variant of hound. The case of the Poitevin is a typical example. These hounds were evolved in the region of Poitiers, in the west of the country, with three distinctive lines in existence at the time of the Revolution.

Selective breeding led not only to hounds with recognisable characteristics, but also to local variants, so that in some cases, members of individual packs have recognisable characteristics.

The most famous were those owned by a Monsieur Larye, which were characterised by their prowess as wolfhounds and distinguished from the Montemboeuf and Céris strains by their tricoloured appearance. After M. Larye became one of the many victims of the guillotine in 1793, his pack was then broken up. Records suggest that after the Revolution, only a couple of his original hounds still survived. They were used as the basis to recreate the original Laryes, but clearly, the strain was no longer the same.

It is reckoned that there were over forty different forms of hound in existence at the outbreak of the Revolution, whereas there are now just 28 recognised breeds for the purposes of venery.

In Britain too, a revolution of a different kind was taking place as the century drew to a close, which was to leave a marked impact on the development of hounds worldwide in the future. For centuries, hunting with hounds had served as a means of procuring food, but now fox hunting had developed into a popular leisure pursuit.

During the early days however, this was a very haphazard event with the hounds themselves varying greatly in appearance and suitability for this task. Havoc often ensued, as not all members of the pack were able to run at the same speed, with some of the hounds displaying more stamina than others. Many hunt masters were actually more concerned with the coloration and appearance of their hounds than their suitability for pursuing foxes, although tricoloured individuals were often favoured, according to some contemporary accounts.

Harriers were frequently pressed into service to hunt foxes but although they could overcome a hare, their ability to run down a fox was often limited. They were simply not able to keep up with its tireless pace. In order to redress the balance, the hunt often began at first light, in the hope of tracking a fox which had recently fed and so would be easier to outrun. Instead, if this plan failed, the hunt could continue through the day until the hounds tired, often allowing the fox to escape. A further disadvantage as far as the hounds were concerned was that they were often coupled together, and so forced to run in pairs.

By the 1750s however, notable changes started to occur, inspired by Hugo Meynell, who lived at Quornden Hall in Leicestershire where he established one of the most famous of all hunts, known simply as the Quorn. Meynell realised that the foxhounds of that era needed to be faster and he set out to breed such hounds. The results of his efforts were considered to be amazing at the time. His foxhounds were soon capable of outpacing stagecoaches which were the fastest mode of transport then known, being able to reach a maximum speed of 13mph (21kph). While the greyhound remained unrivalled as a sprinter, the foxhound was increasingly valued for its stamina.

Meynell's efforts revolutionised fox hunting and served to attract many more devotees, not least because the chase no longer had to begin at first light, thanks to the speed of the hounds. Merken, a foxhound of this era, was carefully timed as completing a four-mile (6.4km) course in just seven minutes, equivalent to over 36mph (57kph).

Other hunts had noted Meynell's achievements in developing the new type of foxhound and followed suit with fierce competition developing between the packs. Not everything went in Hugo Meynell's favour. Large sums of money changed hands when Meynell's hounds lost to those bred by the Hon. John Smith-Barry of the Cheshire Hunt in a drag hunt organised on Newmarket Heath in 1762. The winner, called Bluecap, took just over eight minutes to complete the course, confirming the widespread development of pace which had taken place in the foxhound by this period. This had been matched by faster horses, enabling riders to keep in close contact with the hounds.

The first pedigree records for foxhounds certainly date back to 1717 and provide one of the most detailed insights into the selective breeding of any animal, let alone dogs. Such records help to highlight the most highly regarded foxhounds of the age, but in the past, they were also doubtless used as an invaluable guide for breeding purposes. As a result, some lineages were soon to have a much greater influence on the development of the breed than others, which in turn helped to fix the type or appearance of the hounds more firmly than in the past.

Uniformity in type results in hounds with similar performance capabilities. The bloodlines of the foxhound have been carefully developed for virtually 300 years. They were the first true pedigree dogs.

These new foxhounds differed significantly from their predecessors. Their wide, broad chests provided for good lung capacity, while their broad backs contributed strength and assisted soundness. The rounded shape of the feet helped to ensure a sound grip even on muddy ground, with powerful, straight legs providing propulsive thrust. The head and neck were relatively small, in contrast to the lumbering scenthound of the past, with the tail being bushy.

Such was the emphasis placed on pedigree that by 1820, it was reckoned that about half of all English foxhounds could trace their ancestry back to the legendary Guzman, bred by Meynell, with the remainder being descended from another famous foxhound called Ranter, which had been kept by Lord Yarborough.

Even so, Masters of the Hunt were reluctant to abandon their aesthetic principles, when it came to the coloration of their packs. The tan coloration on the back became inextricably linked with both the Belvoir packs, to the extent that this feature even became christened the 'Belvoir tan'. Even today, coloration remains a significant feature of many hound breeds and serves to reflect their common ancestry.

The significant changes which had taken place during the 18th century meant that there were casualties however, most notably among the older, slower types of hound. Not only had the quarry changed to a large extent, but also the style of hunting. Deer had become very scarce, to the extent that few apart from King George III maintained a pack of buckhounds. His hunts were very formal affairs, and although chased by riders and hounds, the deer were left essentially unharmed, though winded, at the end of the proceedings, and were taken back to the royal deer park so they could recover from their ordeal.

In the countryside at large however, hunting deer, especially illegally, remained a dangerous pursuit, both for man and hound. If caught there was the distinct possibility that the poacher could be sentenced to hang, while tackling a deer, especially a hind with a calf, could be fatal for a dog, particularly one working alone. The hind's feet were quite capable of inflicting a deadly blow, while antlers could also represent serious danger to an unwary hound, or more often a lurcher in these cases.

Lurchers were bred from a combination of hound and working dog stock, with coloration rather than type being vital. A dark coloured individual would have a much greater likelihood of remaining undetected by a keen-eyed gamekeeper at night. Silence was another essential characteristic of these dogs, unlike the baying pack hound: any sound while hunting could spell disaster.

In spite of continuing restrictions on their ownership, lurchers were still widely kept, although often docked to disguise their hunting prowess. Intelligence and responsiveness were key attributes in these dogs, although they varied greatly in appearance, depending on their origins. They were about three-quarters the size of greyhounds, and frequently wire-coated, possessing sufficient pace to catch hares or rabbits.

It was the rising popularity of the gundog however, which helped to curb the influence of poachers and their canine companions. No longer could they hide in the dark, since they were likely to be detected. Cruel though it may seem, gamekeepers invariably sought to kill the lurcher under these circumstances, reflecting the importance of these dogs to their owners on their nightly excursions.

The otterhound – a breed distinguished by the waterproof characteristics of its coat and its swimming abilities.

The 19th century was to mark a number of significant changes in the relationship between people and their dogs, particularly in Britain. Sporting fashion meant that gundogs were in the ascendancy, typically working on a one-to-one basis with their owners. This helped to develop the concept of dogs as individuals, and probably served to assist their changing role from worker to companion on a hitherto unparalleled scale by the close of the century.

Shooting provided better sport, especially since traditional quarry had become exceedingly scarce in some cases. Otterhounds in particular faced an uncertain future because of the severe decline in the numbers of otters in the country. One Midlands pack was dispersed in 1844, after having helped to wipe out otters from the rivers of Staffordshire and neighbouring counties. Only in Cumbria was there still a realistic hope of being able to hunt successfully with such hounds by this time.

The survival of otterhounds through to the present day is perhaps surprising, although their rough-coated appearance is highly impressive. The breed's continued existence was probably assisted by the change from working to companion status, from which many dogs benefited during the latter part of the 19th century. Even so, its hunting prowess was not entirely forgotten either, with eight packs still in existence, when otter hunting was finally outlawed in 1977. Otterhounds were well able to dispatch their potentially dangerous quarry without difficulty, being equipped with exceedingly powerful jaws.

It had been common practice since the 1770s for packs of hounds to be displayed during the late summer, prior to the onset of the hunting season. However, a new urban trend began in the public houses of London which was soon to have a dramatic and lasting impact on the keeping of all dogs.

Charles Aistrop, who was landlord of the *Elephant and Castle* public house in Westminster, started to organise a series of shows for dogs in 1834, as an alternative source of entertainment for customers. He offered a silver cream jug as a prize, and before long his dog shows became a regular event. They continued when he took over as licensee of another pub called *The Eight Bells*. Aistrop himself became secretary of the Toy Spaniel Club and it is clear that in these early days, small dogs, including Italian greyhounds, were prominent at his shows.

Things soon started to change dramatically however, when Aistrop was succeeded in this post by Charles Cruft who had teamed up with an entrepreneur called James Spratt, to market dog food, which was a new concept at that stage. Cruft's travels brought him into contact with a number of wealthy and influential dog owners of the period. His first direct involvement in the running of dog shows had been at the Paris Exhibition of 1878. Back in London, he decided to launch a terrier show, which was held with the support of patrons such as the Duchess of Newcastle at the Royal Aquarium.

It proved to be a success, and encouraged Cruft to launch a more ambitious event in 1891. Ever the showman, he promoted his new show under the banner of Cruft's Great Dog Show, taking advertising in *The Times* newspaper to announce that visitors could expect the finest exhibition of dogs from around the world.

Needless to say, this was rather an exaggeration, but the growing and affluent Victorian middle class supported the show enthusiastically. Cruft's greatest success however, was to persuade Queen Victoria herself to enter some of her beloved Pomeranians at his show, and then to ensure that they were amongst the winners.

There were only seven breeds of hound to be seen at this show however, in spite of Cruft's proud boast that all breeds from around the world would be on view. The largest entry comprised 47 dachshunds, followed by 36 borzois, a breed that had attracted considerable interest because of its associations with both the British and Russian royal families.

Among the surprises was the fact that although there were 30 deerhounds, no Irish wolfhounds were entered for this show. Whippets just outnumbered greyhounds by 23 to 19 and 24 bloodhounds were on view as well. The basset hound, which was a relatively new breed in Britain at that time, perhaps not surprisingly had the smallest entry, comprised of just 13

Dachshunds waiting to enter the ring. Dog shows attract a large following today and have helped to establish many hound breeds as household companions.

individuals, including some rough-coated bassets in this total.

Although Cruft's show was ultimately to develop into an event of international renown, thanks in part to his showmanship, there were detractors in those early days. The entries in the sporting section including hounds were not considered to be as good as at various Kennel Club events, but Cruft was a shrewd commercial operator. When he moved to the Agricultural Halls in Islington, he negotiated a contract which meant that others intending to promote any dog shows in the capital over the course of several years were to be denied access to this premier venue.

It was perhaps because Cruft was not a dog man himself that perversely, his shows attained the greatest commercial success, capturing the public imagination with his style of presentation. He appreciated the value of making it easy for people to travel with their dogs, and he even prepared a special design of carriage for this purpose. By 1903, his show was so firmly established that he was able to negotiate with the railway companies to ensure that those attending the show received discounted fares.

There was a huge growth in dog ownership during the last quarter of the 19th century, which undoubtedly benefited Cruft's show. C.H. Lane, writing at the turn of the century, recorded that the canine population had grown fifty-fold during this period. Although this may have been an exaggeration, there is no doubt that this era marked the start of the rise of the dog as a companion.

New breeds also started to attract attention, particularly borzois, also known as Russian or Siberian wolfhounds, in the case of the hound breeds. The basset hound too was growing in popularity, as was the grand griffon Vendéen, a French hound which soon faded from the scene, although in recent years, the petit basset griffon Vendéen has re-emerged on the international scene.

Some hound breeds such as the borzoi have built up an international following, largely as a result of their appearance at dog shows, whereas others remain very localised in distribution.

One of the features of Cruft's early shows was the way in which dogs were brought from overseas, before quarantine for fear of rabies became *de rigueur*. At the 1892 show, there was keen competition in the hound section between Koratai, a British-based borzoi owned by a Mr Muir and a team sent from Russia itself by the Tsar, the Grand Duke Nicholas and Prince Constantine of Oldenbourg. Even the Kennel Club's rather critical report of this event could not fail to comment on the quality of these hounds and highlighted the difficulty of the judge's task, which saw Koratai emerge victorious.

The following year could have spelt disaster for Cruft's whole enterprise however, because of another group of borzois brought from Russia by Mr E. Block. He appears to have been trying to cash in on the demand for these elegant hounds, but unfortunately, a number of them were suffering from distemper. Although this viral ailment still remains a potential killer today, show dogs and household pets are routinely vaccinated against it. In 1892 however, its highly infectious nature meant that an epidemic could be spread as the result of a sick individual being brought to a show.

Cruft did employ a veterinary surgeon to carry out inspections at his event, but in this case,

Characteristic differences have often arisen between hounds kept for hunting purposes, and those of the same breed bred for the show ring.

although disbarred, the borzois still somehow managed to gain admittance to the show. Rumours were rife, with the suggestion being made that one had actually died on the bench in the show hall.

This particular show was the first which Cruft operated under the rules of the Kennel Club and they insisted on carrying out an investigation into the incident. There were already misgivings within the Kennel Club about the way in which Cruft was popularising his shows, in comparison with their own, and resentment at the fact that they could no longer use the Agricultural Halls, because of Cruft's monopolistic arrangement with the organisers.

Cruft's defence was that the borzois had managed to avoid his inspection process, and he emphasised that over 40 dogs in total had been denied access to the show. The Kennel Club were not surprisingly unimpressed by this explanation, blaming Cruft and his failure to provide a hospital area for dogs suspected of being ill. They stopped short of withdrawing their approval for his shows however, perhaps not wishing to become embroiled in what would certainly have become a bitter and highly publicised dispute. Instead, the Kennel Club imposed rule changes which meant that Cruft himself, as Show Executive, would be responsible for overseeing the rules were correctly adhered to in the future. This was a small price to pay for their continued support.

Although Cruft's show came to dominate the public image of dog shows in Britain, achieving worldwide status, similar events were being staged in other countries. The American Kennel Club (AKC) was formed during 1884, operating on similar lines to the British model. Beginning in 1863, the Société d'Acclimation in France started to hold regular shows which proved to be highly successful. The Société Centrale pour l'Amélioration des Races de Chiens en France was then to set up in 1884, and acted as a major catalyst in promoting shows. Hounds benefited accordingly, with their long history helping to ensure that they were already of a fairly high standard by this stage.

There was a clear tendency emerging however, towards smaller companion dogs, which accelerated after the First World War with the break-up of many of the large estates where hunting had been a popular pastime for centuries. Those hounds which settled well in the home as pets continued to grow in popularity, particularly the smooth-coated dachshund, whereas the otterhound continued to decline in numbers.

Growing concern for animal welfare meant that there was increasing opposition to hunting. As a means of encouraging the speed of greyhounds, but without the necessity of having to provide them with live hares, an American engineer called Owen Smith devised the concept of greyhound racing. The hounds would compete against each other by chasing a lure, in the form of a mechanical hare, around a track. The hare would run on a rail, and its speed could be adjusted to that of the chasing greyhounds.

In the early days, a number of different hound breeds were pitted against the hare in this way, but it soon became apparent that greyhounds were most adaptable for this purpose. As with horse racing, there are events run over differing distances. The hare serves as a lure for the dogs. Although it is not scented in any way, it draws them in the same way that a pet hound will chase after a ball. Should a greyhound reach the hare for any reason, it will seek to seize it. Other sighthounds are not generally raced, but Afghan hounds are sometimes encouraged to run against each other on the track.

The number of different hounds being kept for show as distinct from hunting or racing purposes has grown greatly during the 20th century, thanks in part to Cruft's shows. The basenji attracted great interest when two examples of the breed were first exhibited at the 1937 event, as an era drew to a close. Charles Cruft died in September 1938, and although his wife ran Cruft's the following year, the war then intervened. It was not until 1948 that the exhibition started again, organised by the Kennel Club which had moved to purchase the show in the interim.

There are some interesting comparisons to be drawn about the way in which the number of breeds on view had grown from the start. At the 1891 show, there had been 45 breeds, of which 32 were of British origin. By 1928, the number on view had risen to 84, and included 33 whose origins lay overseas.

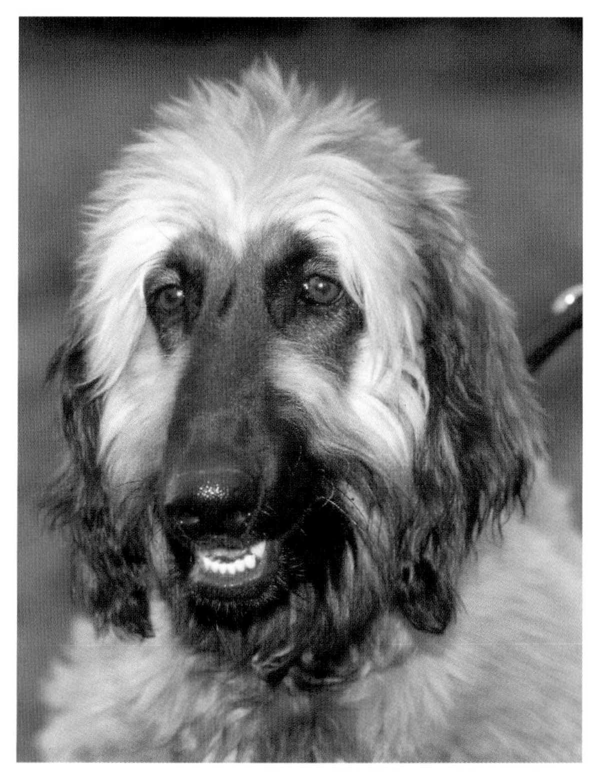

The Afghan is one breed which has changed dramatically following its appearance in the show ring, gaining a far more profuse coat.

This growing international influence has greatly expanded entries within the hound group. Afghan hounds for example, are now always well-represented at Cruft's and other major shows around the globe. Fashion undeniably plays a part in determining the respective popularity of breeds. Although the number of smooth-haired dachshunds may have declined from a peak at the 1948 show, where over 336 were entered, other breeds have quickly built up a strong following. The Pharaoh hound, perhaps surprisingly, was essentially unknown outside its native Malta until 1970. None of these hounds were registered with the Kennel Club, yet such was the tremendous level of interest in them that within five years, they had attained championship status in Britain and could be seen in the Miscellaneous Class at American Kennel Club shows.

Another breed which has grown greatly in popularity on the international scene in recent years is the petit basset griffon Vendéen. Worldwide, it is now almost certainly the most widely kept of the French hounds.

Breeds become fashionable on occasion, as happened in the case of the Pharaoh hound following its introduction to the show scene in the 1970s.

Those breeds of hound which are popular internationally have attained this status in the 20th century as the result of the growth of interest in dog showing, rather than as hunting dogs. They have altered, often quite significantly in appearance as a result, being developed from a primarily aesthetic rather than functional viewpoint. This is quite marked in the case of the Afghan hound, where the coat of today's champions is far longer and more profuse than that of their ancestors, while physically the exhibition greyhound has diversified markedly from its track counterpart.

There are still some hounds however, which have not gained great popularity, and yet still enjoy a dedicated following in those areas where they evolved. In France especially, there are a number of breeds which remain essentially unknown outside their area of origin, but perhaps this applies even more in the USA, where certain hounds are still unlikely to be encountered outside their state of origin.

Breeding for exhibition purposes inevitably depends on hound fanciers being able to find homes among pet seekers for many of their puppies. The majority of a litter will inevitably not be suitable for show purposes because of minor defects, and so if a breed is to attain any level of popularity, it must build up support amongst the wider dog-owning public as well. The genial nature of hounds has helped to ensure their popularity, in spite of their rather wayward natures on occasions. They have crossed the threshold after centuries in the kennels, to become true companions, appreciated by young and old alike.

Chapter 5
The Hounds of Britain, Ireland and France

The relatively large number of hound breeds associated with these countries reflects their long tradition of hunting. Although the ancestors of today's greyhounds may have evolved originally in the Middle East, it has been in Britain that the breed has been developed since Roman times. Their name may be a corruption of the word 'gazehound', because of the way in which they hunt by sight. This is not the only possibility however, since alternatively, it might be derived from the old English word 'greg', which simply meant 'dog'.

There is no doubt that greyhound-type dogs were common from the earliest stages of canine history, helping to explain the development of their name. Dr Caius proposed that it came from 'gradus' or 'gre' meaning 'first among dogs', although another alternative was that it was of Greek origin, reflecting the ancient ancestry of these hounds. Certainly, the name 'greyhound' was in widespread usage in Britain by the sixteenth century, with Shakespeare mentioning the breed in both the *Merry Wives of Windsor* and *Henry V*.

The greyhound is the best-known sighthound in the world today, and represents a lineage that has changed relatively little down the centuries.

Although the smooth, short coat of the greyhound is a distinctive feature of the breed today, a rough-coated form has been recorded as far back as Greek times. Arrian, who lived in the reign of the Emperor Hadrian (138–76 BC) described both varieties, with the former being most common and widely-used for coursing.

In more recent times, greyhounds have become inextricably linked with the coursing event known as the Waterloo Cup. The origins of this event date back to 1825, when the Earl of Sefton and Viscount Molyneux established the Altcar Club, which met at the Waterloo Hotel in Liverpool. The first winner of this event was a red bitch called Milanie, owned by Viscount Molyneux. His father, Lord Sefton, who helped to pioneer the event did not actually participate directly until 1880, when he won with his own dog, called Senate.

The vagaries of life and luck have been evident in the winners of the Waterloo Cup, particularly during the 1890s. Colonel North paid the huge sum of 890 guineas to purchase a brindled greyhound called Fullerton for the event, and was duly rewarded, lifting the cup for four years in succession, from 1889–1892. Yet shortly afterwards, a bitch called Fabulous Fortune won the event, after being discovered lying in front of the fire in a public house in Brampton, and purchased for less than £1!

The popularity of coursing during that era was such that when the National Coursing Club decreed that all entrants had to be registered from 15 July 1883, details of nearly a thousand greyhounds were submitted. It would appear that brindle forms were quite scarce at this time, compared with black or black and white individuals, based on the entries in the first stud book.

In Ireland too, coursing attained considerable popularity, with the establishment of the Brownlow Cup in 1859, under Lord Lurgan's organisation. A split with the National Coursing Club then took place in 1916, as a result of the formation of the Irish Coursing Club. Before long however, the use of greyhounds in another guise was bringing a whole new sporting dimension to their athletic ability.

Greyhound racing had begun in the USA, following the development of the mechanical line in 1912 by Owen Patrick Smith. He then set up the first greyhound track at Emeryville, California, and the popularity of the sport grew to such an extent that by 1918, Smith owned 25 tracks across the USA.

It was not long before greyhound racing was introduced to Europe. The Greyhound Racing Association was set up in Manchester, England, and here the first track was established at Belle Vue, opening on 24 July 1926. The equally famous White City track, located at Shepherd's Bush in London, was developed in the following year, and the National Greyhound Racing Club (NGRC) which oversees the sport was then founded in January 1928.

Although training systems obviously differ, greyhound puppies may start running over short distances against each other soon after weaning. Training typically begins in earnest once the dogs are approximately six months of age. Soon after, they are encouraged to pursue a drag lure, and from 18 months old, the young greyhounds will make their first appearance at a race track.

One of the most famous of all greyhounds, who left an indelible mark on racing, actually never appeared on the track. The greyhound in question was Mutton Cutlet, who was descended from coursing stock. When he died in 1934, he had sired more than 500 winners, both on the track and at coursing events. Among his male progeny was Beef Cutlet, who was possibly the fastest greyhound in history. In turn, he sired both Juvenile Classic, a winning hurdler, and Junior Classic.

The Greyhound Derby, run at the White City track each year, remains the premier event in the European greyhound racing calendar. In total, there are eight such Classics, which attract the top greyhounds, run at various British tracks. In the USA, the Greyhound Race of Champions, which was first run in 1982, is considered to be the premier challenge, although there are a number of other similar events, such as the American Derby, held at Lincoln, Rhode Island.

Improvements not only in the technology, giving better track surfaces and more accurate time-keeping, but also in the breeding of the greyhounds themselves since the inception of this sport have resulted in improved track times.

Greyhound racing has developed into a major industry, both on and off the course, since it began in the USA during the early 1900s.

When perhaps the most famous racing greyhound ever known, Mick the Miller, won the Derby at the White City track in 1929, it took him 29.96 seconds to cover the 525yd (480m) course. The 29-second barrier was then broken in 1947 for the first time at this event, when Trev's Perfection clocked 28.95 seconds – over a second faster.

In the USA, where heats are typically comprised of up to a dozen dogs, extending over courses measuring from 5/16ths to 9/16ths of a mile, the oldest record still standing, in terms of time, only dates back to 1987, reflecting the continuing progress of the greyhound as an athlete. The greyhound is unique among all breeds of domestic dog in not suffering from hip dysplasia, a weakness of the ball and socket joint at the top of the hind legs, which results in partial, even severe lameness in affected individuals.

Many greyhound racing enthusiasts prefer to own a male dog rather than a bitch, simply because the dog can be entered in more races, while bitches obviously cannot be raced when they are in season. Bitches are therefore often cheaper to purchase, but a female winner will still be valuable for breeding purposes, although successful male greyhounds are highly sought after at stud.

Most greyhounds that are sound performers on the track will peak during their third or fourth year, being retired for breeding purposes soon afterwards. Males can then enjoy a potentially long career at stud, with Beef Cutlet and Mick the Miller for example both living to over twelve years of age.

It is not easy to pick out a potential winner from a litter, although the puppy's movement, in turn reflecting its pace, will be critical. Size is far less significant – bitches, in spite of being considerably smaller than male dogs, are not significantly disadvantaged. Rebel Light, winner of the Irish Coursing Derby in 1940, was double the weight of Alvaston Lulu Belle, who weighed just 45lb (20kg) and yet was one of the most successful racing greyhounds of all time.

A high percentage of greyhounds intended for racing do fail to make the grade however, and many of these are found homes as pets. Greyhounds have gentle natures, and while older dogs of this type can be nervous at first, they will soon settle well in domestic surroundings. One of the popular myths however, which can hamper homing programmes, is that they require a lot of exercise. In fact, as is apparent from track events, which often last less than 30 seconds, they are sprinters rather than endurance runners.

A quick circuit around the park will suffice for them, but there is a potential risk that they could perceive a smaller dog such as a Yorkshire terrier as an elusive hare which they never outpaced on the track! As a result, all greyhounds should be muzzled in a park or public place when let off the leash, to prevent any unfortunate encounters of this type. Greyhounds are capable of outpacing any other dog, attaining a top speed of roughly 45.5mph (73kph), which also makes it virtually impossible to catch one when it starts to sprint off into the distance.

The long stride of the greyhound contributes to its pace, with the major propulsive thrust coming from its powerful hindquarters.

Type is considered to be even more important in the case of a show greyhound, compared with a racing or coursing dog. Judging standards are tightly prescribed, to the extent that there is much more uniformity in the show ring, although no restrictions are placed on the colours or combinations that can be exhibited. Greyhounds may range in colour from white through shades of cream and fawn to red, blue (which has a greyish hue) and black. Brindles, which are a combination of black and brown, as well as bicolours are also common.

Today, the number of exhibition greyhounds being registered in the UK is lower than it was in the early days following the founding of the Kennel Club in 1873. This is possibly a reflection of the increasing number of breeds within the hound section that are now available. Nevertheless, the breed has done well at Cruft's,

taking the best-in-show award no less than three times, most recently in 1956, making them presently the most successful member of the hound group in this regard.

The Italian greyhound is derived from the same ancestral stock as its larger, better known relative, although it is typically regarded as a toy breed rather than a true hound. These small dogs may first have been kept by the Romans, being known today in Italy as Piccoli Levrieri Italiani. Much of their subsequent development has taken place elsewhere in Europe. Italian greyhounds were popular companions with the wealthy, over the course of many years, often being seen at royal courts where they were favoured as ladies' companions. Anne of Denmark and Mary Queen of Scots were among the breed's devotees.

The quiet nature of these dogs (a characteristic shared with their larger relatives) is reputed to have saved the Prussian ruler Frederick the Great (1712–86) during the Seven Years War. He was briefly forced to take refuge under a bridge with his favourite Italian greyhound to avoid being discovered by enemy soldiers. Should the dog have barked, it would have betrayed their position, with devastating consequences.

During the Victorian era in Britain, there was an increasing tendency to miniaturise these greyhounds even further. Constantly mating the smallest and often related examples together ultimately led to a loss of soundness and a high degree of infertility became associated with the breed.

The situation began to improve with the founding of the Italian Greyhound Club in 1900, which sought to remedy the problems. The numbers of these dogs subsequently fell as a result of the Second World War, but the introduction of new stock from North America led to a revival in their numbers. Today's Italian greyhounds typically measure between 13–15in (33–38cm) at the shoulder, and weigh 6–8lb (2.7–3.6kg) on average, although slightly larger individuals can be up to 10lb (4.5kg).

As with greyhounds, their coats are thin and glossy, which, coupled with a lack of body fat, leaves them especially vulnerable to the cold. Provided they are fitted with a suitable coat when outdoors during periods of bad weather however, Italian greyhounds are not especially delicate dogs. They are very responsive though, and will react accordingly if scolded. Their athletic build means that they should have the opportunity to run off the leash each day. Unlike the case with their larger relatives, brindles are not acceptable for exhibition purposes, neither are blue or black individuals with tan markings.

A fusion of greyhound and Italian greyhound blood probably contributed to the development of the whippet, whose origins lie in the north of England. This breed became known affectionately as the working man's racehorse, since whippets were kept initially for racing purposes by miners, as well as for occasional rabbiting. The races were held across open stretches of ground, rather than set tracks, which meant that unlike greyhounds, the whippet ran on the straight and not a circuit. Whippets have great acceleration, which enables them to cover a course of 150yd (137m) in just 8 seconds – equivalent in speed to nearly 37mph (58kph).

Smooth-coated whippets are much more common than their rough-coated counterparts.

Although terrier crosses are also said to have contributed to the whippet's development, this is certainly not apparent from the breed's physical appearance today. It is possible however, that some crosses with the Bedlington terrier, which hails from the same north-eastern part of England and is also built for pace, could have occurred on occasions in the past. Both share the characteristic roach back, which contributes to the power when they run, being coupled to the powerful hindquarters. The whippet's feet are also well adapted to maintain a good grip, with the strong pads helping to act as effective shock absorbers as well. The deep chest provides for good lung capacity, to meet the demands of the circulatory system.

Whippets sometimes give the impression of being nervous, by keeping their long, tapering tail tucked down beneath their hind legs. This is a normal posture when resting however, with the tail then being carried in an upward curve once the dog starts to run, although it does not extend actually over the back.

In terms of temperament, there are few hounds, or indeed dogs in general, which are better suited to being household pets. They are ideal companions in a home with children, being tolerant and friendly, while their obedient nature makes this breed an ideal choice for the novice exhibitor of any age. The whippet was first recognised by the Kennel Club in 1902, having made its debut at Cruft's five years earlier. The range of colours is similar to those associated with the greyhound, although paler shades such as fawn tend to be most popular.

The whippet was originally taken to the USA in the early 1900s, by textile workers from Lancashire who settled in New England. Since then, the breed has established a strong following throughout the country, both on the track and in the show ring. Whippets today are raced after an electric lure, in a similar fashion to greyhounds. This is far removed from the earliest days of the sport when owners encouraged their dogs along the track from the winning post by waving rags at them, which is why whippets acquired the

The deep chest of the whippet provides for good lung capacity, with the broad back reinforcing the power from the hindquarters.

Built for speed, the whippet is a sprinter, rather than a long-distance runner. It is a very graceful hound.

unusual name 'rag dogs'. The straight front legs of the breed stay close to the ground, enabling them to run in an apparently effortless fashion.

In terms of stature, the American show standard calls for a slightly taller dog than would be acceptable in the UK. During the early days of the whippet's development, there were actually two coat variants – rough and smooth – in existence, but in due course, the latter took over, to the extent that today, rough coated whippets are rare and unrecognised for exhibition purposes. They are still to be seen occasionally however, often at lurcher events.

Lurchers as a group are also unrecognised by the main show bodies, since these dogs do not conform to any standard in terms of appearance. Their ancestry can also be very variable, although such dogs have been kept in rural areas of Britain and Ireland for many centuries. It is hard to assess the numbers of lurchers today with any degree of certainty, but it has been suggested that the number in Britain alone could exceed over 5,000 individuals.

During recent years there have been moves by lurcher enthusiasts to establish these dogs on a more formal basis. The first show for lurchers was held in 1971, at Lambourn in Berkshire, with both judging and racing heats now being firmly established as a feature of such events. The name 'lurcher' derives from the old Romany (gypsy) dialect, with the word 'lur' meaning 'thief', and so describing the use of these hound crosses to catch game illicitly in the company of poachers.

Lurchers are the product of crosses between sighthounds and sheepdogs with a male dog of the former group typically being mated with a bitch of the latter type. It is usually preferable to select dogs of similar coloration, with darker individuals traditionally being favoured since they were less likely to be detected in the dark.

Today however, a much wider range of colours has been created, as the result of combinations such as red and white whippets mated with tricoloured Shetland sheepdogs (often known affectionately as 'Shelties'). The puppies resulting from whippet crosses will feature in the smaller of the two lurcher categories which have been established – those which are under 22in (65cm) in height at the withers. Larger lurchers are the result of greyhound or deerhound crosses, in place of the whippet, while larger sheepdogs, such as the rough collie may also be favoured in place of the Shetland sheepdog.

Certain crosses are traditionally favoured in particular areas, with deerhound stock being more commonly used in Scotland for example. Since the resulting puppies are of course fertile, there is scope for further refinement in the second generation. It is not uncommon for further sighthound blood to be introduced at this stage, with lurchers being mated to sighthounds, as a means of seeking to improve their pace. The parentage of the resulting puppies is then often described as 0.75 sighthound plus 0.25 sheepdog. On occasions, especially during recent times, foreign breeds have been used in the breeding of lurchers, including salukis and Afghan hounds, but the traditional crossings still retain the strongest support.

Lurchers differ from longdogs by virtue of their breeding, although the description of lurcher is sometimes used as an all-embracing term, for both groups. Longdogs, in comparison with lurchers, are true hounds, albeit of cross-bred origin. Typical longdogs are the product of matings between deerhounds and greyhounds for example, although the value of such crosses is controversial.

One area where longdogs of this type usually excel is in terms of their coat, which is frequently rough, reflecting their deerhound ancestry, rather than smooth like a greyhound's. This means they are more suited to working outside when the weather is wet and cold. These crossbreds are also better at hare coursing than lurchers, simply because they are faster and tend to be more agile, as a result of their pure sighthound origins, although their large size, especially in the case of male dogs, can restrict their ability to turn in tight circles.

Crosses between whippets and greyhounds have traditionally been favoured for hare hunting purposes, with the largest whippets being preferred for this task. These strong dogs were especially popular after the Second World War for a time, in Gloucestershire and the Cotswold area of England, but they are not often encountered today.

Although less popular than greyhound racing today, whippet racing still has its devotees. During the last century, the whippet became known as the 'poor man's racehorse', because of its racing abilities.

Undoubtedly the most controversial of the longdogs are those of saluki–greyhound origins. They are most likely to be encountered in parts of Britain where the ground is relatively flat and open, mimicking the terrain where salukis (see page 23) naturally occur. Unfortunately, the natural stamina of the saluki is such that even such crosses are hard to control. Since these characteristics have been incorporated into the resulting hybrids, longdogs of this type can therefore run for much longer than pure greyhounds.

If ever there was confusion between longdogs and lurchers however, the saluki-greyhound cross emphasises the difference. Through history, lurchers have been kept for poaching purposes, working silently and yet in close contact with their owners, proving to be exceedingly biddable. In contrast, saluki–greyhound longdogs are free spirits, congenitally incapable of behaving in this fashion! Their pace and stamina is highly valued by enthusiasts however, who are prepared to overlook this deficiency.

The gulf that has grown up between longdogs and lurchers as a group and the show stock of their ancestors in recent years is well exemplified by the case of the deerhound. In many cases, it has been those individuals which had poor conformation from the perspective of the show standard that have been used as the basis for longdog/lurcher breeding.

Although the deerhound is now inextricably linked with Scotland it is probably not indigenous to this area, with its ancestors having been brought here between the 5th and 2nd centuries BC by the Celts. Although the similarity may not be immediately apparent, there is a distinct resemblance in profile between this breed and the greyhound, to the extent that they might even have a common ancestry. This theory is reinforced by the fact that the Celts had invaded areas of the Middle East where greyhound-type dogs were almost certainly kept, helping to explain their transposition from here to Scotland.

The original hounds were probably smooth-coated, being crossed with native wiry-haired dogs to improve their hardiness in the relatively cold and damp surroundings of their new homeland. Aside from its coat, the deerhound of today is now slightly larger than the greyhound, and proportionately more powerful. Having been evolved for hunting over rough terrain, it also displays greater stamina.

Up until the 18th century, ownership of deerhounds was linked inextricably with the highland chieftains, to the extent that the law forbade anyone below the rank of earl from owning one of these hounds. The disintegration of the existing hierarchy which followed the defeat of the Scottish by the English at the Battle of Culloden in 1745, combined with other changes in society then threatened the continued existence of the breed. No longer was it essential to hunt deer with dogs, as firearms meant that they could be killed effectively by careful stalking. Changing land use patterns also imposed increasing restrictions on the area available for hunting, thanks to increasing deforestation and fencing of agricultural land.

By the time that two brothers Duncan (Lord Colonsay) and Archibald McNeill began to seek to restore the breed to its former glory in the 1820s, the numbers of these hounds had plummeted, particularly in eastern Scotland. But the Colonsay revival, as this period in the deerhound's history has been dubbed, attracted influential support. The Scottish Deerhound Club was established in 1891, with the breed gaining the patronage of Queen Victoria, while the famous artist Landseer chose to feature deerhounds in a number of his works, set against the background of a roaring fire in the confines of a Scottish castle.

His reputation ensured that the breed would be drawn to public attention through such portrayals. Deerhounds did not lack support from the writers of the day either, with Sir Walter Scott not only featuring the breed in his novels, but also owning a bitch called Marda which he was to describe as 'the most perfect creature of heaven'.

The breed standard was drawn up in 1892, and by this stage, the deerhound was gaining in popularity in North America as well. There had been nine entries at the inaugural Westminster Kennel Club show (which holds an equivalent position to Cruft's in the North American dog calendar). These deerhounds included two that were from Queen Victoria's own kennels and priced accordingly, at the huge sum of £10,000 each.

For show purposes, these hounds need relatively little grooming, with their shaggy, weather-resistant coat feeling harsh to the touch, being softer on the head and underparts. Paler coloured deerhounds such as yellow or red fawn with black points on the ears and muzzle were favoured by the McNeills, but dark blue-grey individuals are often considered to display the best quality in terms of the show standard today. Males are significantly larger and heavier than bitches, and the neck in all cases should be particularly muscular. This reflects the strength that these hounds required in order to wrestle a stag to the ground, and the nape should be prominent as well.

During the Second World War, the numbers of deerhounds again fell quite significantly in Europe, mainly because of the difficulties kennel owners encountered in obtaining adequate food for these large dogs. Today, although not especially numerous they are reasonably common again, particularly in their homeland. As with other sighthounds, the deerhound is very quiet by nature, and although good periods of exercise are essential, they will settle down well in the confines of a home, growing to be loyal companions if not dedicated guard dogs. In North America, these hounds are described as Scottish deerhounds, rather than simply as deerhounds.

Staghounds in contrast are a very different type of hound, which have never found their way into the show ring, being kept entirely in packs for hunting purposes. The last remaining pack, kept by the North Devon Hunt, pursued red deer on the forests of Exmoor in the south-west of England up until 1825.

These hounds were then purchased by a Mr Charles Shard who lived at Somborne House in Hampshire. The terrain in this more easterly region of the country was less satisfactory however, with the staghounds sustaining bad injuries to their paws because of the flinty ground. As a result, Mr Shard sold the pack to Germany late in 1826, and to some enthusiasts who resided in the vicinity of Epping Forest.

A contemporary portrait of a couple of these North Devon staghounds, published in 1826, reveals them to have been strong, powerful short-coated dogs, with the male dog being larger than the bitch. They apparently were often yellow and white in colour, standing up to 26in (65cm) tall. Their noses were quite broad, revealing a scent-hound nature and they bore a closer similarity to a foxhound than a deerhound, although they were clearly more powerful, in line with their quarry.

While nothing appears to be known about the fate of the surviving staghounds once this pack was divided up, it is clear that the influence of these hounds continued through the harrier lineage in their native area. The harriers kept by Mr Fronde during the late 1840s were among those descended from North Devon staghound stock, as reflected in part by their coloration.

The hounds used for deer hunting in Britain in more recent years have been derived essentially from foxhound stock. The division of hounds kept for hunting deer into staghounds and buckhounds dates back at least to the reign of Henry III (1216–1272), but surviving packs now face an exceedingly uncertain future, with the severe curtailment of deer hunting with hounds in Britain. A number have already been destroyed and other hunts will inevitably adopt a similar policy if the hounds are not wanted elsewhere in Europe. These hounds are kennelled and have been used entirely for hunting purposes, making them unsuitable for life in the domestic environment.

The origins of the Welsh hound date back nearly as far, being described by Edward, Prince of Wales in 1304. Such hounds were kept for hunting hares, being descended at least in part from the old Southern hound. One particular distinctive feature of the Welsh hound was its crooked legs, which nevertheless did not appear to handicap its ability in the field. Down the centuries, a range of other hounds have been introduced to Welsh bloodlines, even French breeds, notably the Bresse hound. The Count de Canteleu described a number of similarities between these two types of hound ranging from their rough coated, black and yellowish appearance to their bell-like voices and excellent scenting skills.

There is also a well-founded link back to the old North Devon staghounds, and it transpires that when this pack was sold, Parson Jack Russell (after whom the terrier breed is named) somehow acquired three bitches which in due course passed to a keen breeder of Welsh hounds, called John Dillwyn Llewelyn. Subsequently his hounds were incorporated into many other packs, and almost certainly, it is the staghound influence which has led to the occasional taller Welsh hound cropping up in some litters.

The more typical size of these hounds is undoubtedly advantageous in the terrain in which they hunt. Much of the landscape is hilly and often densely wooded, and hounds which can run up the steep slopes must have hocks that are relatively close to the ground, to provide ease of movement under these circumstances. Keen scenting skills and a loud voice are other necessary attributes for hounds kept for hunting purposes in this type of countryside.

Similar attributes are apparent in Fell hounds, which originate from the Lake District in the north-west of England, where the ground is often even steeper and more craggy in parts. Slipping under these circumstances could be fatal, and so sound feet are an essential attribute. These hounds have elongated hare-shaped feet therefore, with their dew claws being left intact to provide a further point of anchorage.

As in the case of the Welsh hound, the hocks are well let down, while the shoulders are equally well laid back, to provide both shock absorption and speed. In many cases, pack members have to pursue foxes on their own, being out of reach of the huntsmen. A loud voice, and pale, often white coloration means that the progress of the hounds can be followed more easily.

The Fell hound, like the Welsh, remains virtually unknown outside its home area, although the Welsh hound has played a significant role in the development of the otterhound. This latter breed has managed to survive and become established internationally, while its traditional quarry has become a protected species.

King John (1199–1216) numbered Master of the Otterhounds among the many titles which he

An otterhound (left) and a wolfhound (right) together. Hounds were developed originally to hunt particular quarry, and differed much more widely in appearance.

could dispense, with contemporary accounts suggesting that otters were a major menace to fresh water fish stocks at a time when these were a vital source of food for the populace in general. Specially trained dogs and handlers were employed by the crown to hunt otters around the country.

For many years, otterhounds were not of fixed type, with whatever dogs proved suitable being used for this task. The royal pack was maintained for over 500 years. Even after the Restoration, Charles II (1660–1685) had a pack of otterhounds.

Towards the late 1800s however, otter hunting with hounds had developed more into a social pastime rather than being a necessity. Contemporary records suggest that there were at least 20 packs which hunted regularly, between April and September when other forms of hunting were not in season.

Perhaps not surprisingly, it was probably at this stage that greater emphasis began to be placed on the appearance of these hounds, especially as they started to be exhibited at the early dog shows. Contemporary accounts suggest that the original ancestry of the otterhound stems from the old Southern hound, which had keen scenting skills and was of the same ancestral stock as the bloodhound. Welsh hounds then contributed, with the development of the modern otterhound probably stemming from the 1860s, following the introduction of French hounds to the existing packs. It is likely that different packs evolved along different lines during this era.

As a result of the Franco-Prussian War which broke out in 1870, the Count de Canteleu dispatched a number of his griffon de Bresse hounds to Waldron Hill, who was the Master of Otterhounds in East Lothian in Scotland. These rough-coated dogs were very similar to the existing otterhounds in this pack, apart from their coloration.

A more remarkable breeding programme undertaken by the Count entailed the mating of a male griffon with a female wolf. He then subsequently paired the female offspring back to a male hound over two generations, producing offspring that by this stage were seven-eighths pure hound. These too passed into the care of Waldron Hill, who used them as otterhounds with great success, although at other times, he found that they were rather aggressive and uncontrollable.

Subsequently, the Count de Canteleu sent his complete pack of griffon Nivernais to Richard Carnaby Forster in England, as the war situation in Europe worsened. These hounds passed into the care of his step-daughter, Lady Mary Hamilton. Finally, during 1906, they were divided up and sold to various other otterhound packs.

Other French hounds also played a part in the developing lineage of this ancient breed during this era. A griffon Vendéen bitch was used to create the Dumfriesshire otterhound pack in 1889, being mated with a bloodhound. One of the puppies in the resulting litter, christened 'Boatman', a rough coated black and tan dog, subsequently laid the basis for this particular stud.

With so much new blood being introduced to the otterhound lineage at this stage, the appearance of the breed probably altered significantly. Traditionally, otterhounds were equally at home on the land or in water. Their scenting abilities were highly developed, reflecting the contribution of the bloodhound to the breed's ancestry. On land, an otterhound could detect the scent or drag made by its quarry over 12 hours earlier, while the endurance of these hounds was such that they could follow the otter's wash for as long as five hours.

The otterhound's webbed feet, coupled with its water-resistant oily coat aid its swimming ability, with the undercoat also providing insulation in cold environments. The breed has a rather shambling gait when walking, followed by an active trot. Once galloping however, the otterhound is able to cover a considerable amount of ground, thanks to its long stride.

The future for the breed looked decidedly uncertain, especially when otter hunting was outlawed in Britain in January 1978. In a bid to ensure the survival of these hounds, the Master of the Kendal and District Otterhounds in the Lake District established a breed club at this stage, which in turn led to a breed standard being accepted by the Kennel Club in 1981.

Lively and affectionate by nature, otterhounds have since enjoyed a more widespread following among dog fanciers, although this is definitely not a breed well suited to urban living. Perhaps surprisingly, otterhounds have been seen in North American show rings for much longer, being exhibited there since 1907. The breed was first introduced to the United States in 1900, and has been kept to hunt a variety of game including mink. Otterhounds in the UK have also been used for this purpose, as a means of curbing these introduced predators. At the time when otter hunting ended, there were just two packs – the Kendal and District and the Dumfriesshire – still in existence, comprising just over 100 hounds in total, but today the future of this breed seems secure.

With moves to ban fox hunting with hounds in Britain, the continued existence of the foxhound is increasingly subject to doubt. Although there have been moves to standardise the breed for show purposes, the vast majority of these hounds are still kept for hunting, as their ancestors have been for hundreds of years. As might be anticipated however, the foxhound is an athletic breed with great stamina, not well-suited to living in anything other than a rural environment. Their instinctive desire to chase, coupled with accompanying training difficulties are also a source of potential problems in the domestic environment, although foxhounds are friendly, well natured dogs. They are also highly social with others of their kind. Their coloration reflects the typical hound colours of black, white and tan in varying degrees, with the markings of pack members being highly individual.

Packs of foxhounds had originally evolved for particular terrain, and even when more widespread appreciation of the development of faster individuals had occurred, it was still not easy in the late 1700s to move hounds for breeding purposes out of their immediate area, compared with the situation today. Hunt masters also erred on the conservative side, not wishing to risk their proven bloodlines in the speculative hope of creating better foxhounds.

The English foxhound is a breed which has not crossed the threshold into the home. These hounds retain strong pack instincts.

It is perhaps not entirely coincidental that those best placed to benefit from combining existing stock lived in the vicinity of the English Midlands. Both Northern and Southern hounds were well known in this region, as well as other breeds such as the Northern beagle.

Ironically perhaps, it appears that foxes were actually much scarcer at the start of the modern fox hunting era than they are today. There was a need for hounds with keen scenting skills, to locate the quarry, while the enthusiasm of the accompanying riders meant that fast pace was also an essential prerequisite among the pack members themselves.

Contemporary illustrations reveal that although the early 19th century foxhounds were significantly smaller in size then those of today, their height was increasing, providing greater stride length as a result and contributing both to their pace and stamina. Those of Belvoir origins were relatively short in stature, indicating the more dominant influence of the Northern beagle, while the Cottesmore was clearly derived to a great extent from taller Southern hound stock. A long neck was also important, indicating a hound with good pace, while the legs were powerful, with the hocks being well let down.

For some, breeding successful foxhounds became an end in itself. One of the most noted breeders of the early Victorian period was Lord Henry Bentinck, although he never hunted with hounds himself. He took over the Burton Hounds in 1842 and subsequently dedicated himself to improving their pace and stamina. By constantly monitoring the progress of individuals in the pack, he was able to pick out those which excelled in the qualities for which he was searching.

Although light boned, they had excellent conformation and played an important part later in the further development of other packs. Gradually however, support switched to heavier boned hounds, although ultimately this was to prove detrimental in many cases.

The individuality seen within packs of foxhounds lasted up until the outbreak of the First World War, which was to be the forerunner to significant social change in Britain, contributing to the break-up of the great estates. Some packs, such as the Badminton, had been noted for their coloration, whereas others, like Lord Fitzhardinge's Berkeley, were highly regarded for their tracking skills and cry.

As packs became more valued for the size and coloration of the foxhounds, so their hunting abilities diminished to a degree, as the craze for the Belvoir tan swept the country. The characteristic 'cry' allowing the hounds to keep in touch – essential for the cohesiveness of the pack – started to disappear, in spite of the fact that they could run faster.

In the border area however, between England and Wales, as well as in Wales itself, traditional hunting virtues were still upheld. Packs in this region were comprised either of pure Welsh hound blood or represented a fusion of English and Welsh stock. The Welsh hound still has a very distinctive appearance, which sets it apart from other British breeds, with a characteristic rough coat, which may be a feature inherited from the ancient Celtic hound. Records suggest that the ancestors of the Welsh hound were brought to the Abbey of Margam in the south-west of Wales, being given as gifts by visiting monks from Normandy and Brittany. The Bresse hound is one French breed which almost certainly played a significant role in its early development.

Although originally kept for deer hunting, crossings with Fell hounds from the north-west of England and foxhounds then modified the hunting skills of the Welsh hound, and increasingly, it became valued for fox-hunting purposes. Even today though, the coloration of the Welsh hound is quite distinctive, often being much lighter than that of the English foxhound which hints at the involvement of French hound blood in its past. Individuals may be predominantly white in colour, with pale lemon coloration confined mainly to the ears and back.

The Welsh hound managed to outlive the closure of the monasteries that took place during the reign of Henry VIII, thanks to the patronage of the local nobility. In fact, the original kennel at Margam Abbey was maintained until th 19th century. Although it has survived and changed both in form and function down the centuries, the Welsh hound still remains virtually unknown outside its homeland.

The type of the English foxhound varies slightly even today, depending partly on the area where the pack is located.

The influence of the Welsh foxhound is much more widespread however, by virtue of crossings into English packs. This link is commemorated in the names of some of the most famous of the hounds, such as Glog Nimrod 04 (with the figures indicating the year of birth) whose lineage was continued to Brecon Paragon 1923 and thence to Palmer 1959, one of the hounds which has impacted greatly in the development of the Beaufort pack.

The origins of the harrier, which was developed primarily for hare hunting, also lie in Wales. Edward, Prince of Wales (who later became Edward II) first described these bow-legged hounds in correspondence with King Louis of France, sending him a group for hunting purposes at the start of the 14th century. Careful training of harriers was important, partly to prevent them pursuing sheep, which was a general fault of young hounds, but also to ensure that they were not diverted to deer or foxes. A key distinction between the use of harriers as distinct from foxhounds was that it was not considered especially significant to kill the hare – the quality of the chase itself was what mattered.

Keen scenting skills were therefore a vital attribute of the harrier. Regional differences began to develop by the 17th century however, and remain apparent today. In the north of England, the hare hunting hounds were fast and agile, well able to jump walls and other obstacles while in pursuit of their quarry. Slower, less nimble hounds were favoured elsewhere, with those from the West Country often requiring assistance from the accompanying huntsmen on foot, when they encountered hedges or fences.

Although at that period, little of the land over which packs hunted contained obstructions of this type, it was not long before breeders were seeking to combine the attributes of these distinctive types of harrier. Pure speed had some drawbacks as well, notably that the hounds could lose the scent while running fast, and would then have to regroup accordingly on the trail. This was not a characteristic associated with Southern harriers however, who were so diligent in tracking that their pace meant they were unlikely to catch up with the hare.

The harrier is therefore derived from a variety of breeds, including Northern beagles, which when crossed with the Southern hounds, produced smaller, faster hounds. There was a growing band of opinion by the 19th century however, that preferred to use foxhounds rather than harriers for hare hunting, even though the latter were now recognised in their own right. While the number of packs increased through the latter half of the century, these were based on small foxhound stock.

Today's harriers are kept essentially in packs rather than as companions or for show purposes. A distinctive form, known as the West Country or Somerset harrier is still kept in this part of England, although its precise origins are unclear. Parson Jack Russell describes these harriers as being descended from English staghounds, crossed with original harrier stock now measuring approximately 21in (52.5cm) tall.

Others believe that cross-breeding between local foxhounds and a pack of the grand chien blanc de roi, brought to England at the start of the French Revolution in 1789, underlie their origins. Porcelaine hounds may also have contributed to the West Country harrier's development. They are versatile dogs, with keen scenting skills, being pitched against foxes as well as hares. The French links with the harrier itself extend back much further however, and may underlie its name which is derived from Norman-Saxon, with *harrier* being the term used to describe a non-specialist hunting dog.

The harrier was not the only hound kept for hunting hares, and particularly during the present century, it has been eclipsed to a great extent by the beagle, whose appeal has extended out beyond the hunting field and into the home. The rising popularity of the beagle is perhaps not entirely surprising, since there used to be a small strain, first documented during the reign of Elizabeth I in the sixteenth century. They were said to be so small as to fit into a glove, although the queen had them carried in special panniers as part of her official retinue. On occasions these small hounds would be used for hunting rabbits, although they were more commonly viewed as companions, usually lacking sufficient stamina to pursue their quarry over any distance.

The origins of the beagle are obscure, although similar hunting dogs were first documented during the reign of Henry VIII when an official called the Keeper of the Beagles was employed to look after them. A print from this era, by Johannes Stradanus, who was based in Bruges, Belgium, portrays small hounds which bear a distinct resemblance to contemporary beagles catching a rabbit.

The beagle retained a strong following down the centuries as part of the royal retinue. William III (1689–1702) was an enthusiast for these hounds, with his pack reportedly accompanied by no less than 400 huntsmen on one occasion during 1695. Later George IV rode with beagles on the Sussex Downs in the vicinity of Brighton. It appears that these were relatively large examples of the emerging breed, since apparently their pace made it difficult for the accompanying riders to keep up with them, although this might have been due in part to the relatively steep terrain.

The popularity of the small type of beagle favoured by Queen Elizabeth I subsequently waned, probably because of its lack of sustained hunting prowess, but underwent a revival during the 18th century. Such examples were often dubbed 'pocket beagles' on account of their size and stood less than 10in (25cm) tall. One of the most famous packs of this type was kept by a Mr Crane during the 1850s. These hounds were remarkably consistent in height, all standing approximately 9in (23cm) tall.

By the end of the century however, the trend was towards larger beagles more suited to the rigours of hunting and the miniature form appears to have died out. The same applies in the case of

The individual markings of the hounds in a pack enable them to be identified from some distance away.

the rough-coated form of these hounds, which was actually more highly regarded for its conformation and soundness than its smooth haired counterpart. There appears to be no reason for its disappearance, other than perhaps that the coloration of the smooth coated type was more highly regarded. Certainly, great attention was paid to the markings of these hounds, whether they were in couples or in a pack.

The compact size of the beagle, its pleasant if rather gluttonous nature and melodic voice have helped it to become highly regarded as a pet. The Beagle Club itself was founded in 1890 and the inaugural breed show occurred six years later. During this era, beagles were taken to the United States and rapidly established a strong following, both as hunters of small game ranging from rabbits to squirrels, and as lively companions. The breed has frequently featured within the top ten of all breeds there, based on the numbers registered annually, and it has even held the top position on this chart. Aside from the opportunities in the show ring, there are roughly 3,000 sanctioned field trials held for beagles each year in the USA.

Further publicity for the breed has derived from the Snoopy character created by cartoonist Charles M. Schulz in the 1950s, who is featured in the *Peanuts* comic strip. Beagles have also received publicity of a less welcome kind because of their use as laboratory animals although public opinion has helped in part to reduce the numbers sacrificed in this way each year.

As it has built up such a strong international

following, the beagle's quarry has changed in some cases and tested the bravery of these small hounds. Instead of docile hares, they can find themselves on the trail of big cats such as jaguar in the New World. While traditionally beagles have been hunted in packs, they have also proved versatile in this regard, being quite able to work simply as individuals or in couples, proving determined and alert hunting companions.

The name 'beagle' is believed to be derived from the Celtic word *beagle*, which means 'small'. Back in France during the late 1800s, Baron Gérard started to cross the beagle with its longer legged cousin the harrier. His aim was to improve the pace of the beagle without compromising its superior scenting skills, compared with those of the harrier. The baron's initial attempts resulted in offspring of different sizes being produced, but the type has now been fixed and such hounds are highly valued in their homeland for hunting not just hares or deer, but even wild boar.

Beagle harriers, as the breed has been christened, are mainly tricolour, with tan often being the predominant colour in the coat. They are relatively stocky in appearance and can also be distinguished from French hounds of similar coloration by the position and size of their ears which are set quite high on the head and yet are relatively small, compared with many French breeds.

In Ireland, a much larger type of beagle has existed for many years. The Kerry beagle is named after the region of the country where it was developed. Its origins are likely to date back to at least the 1500s and possibly earlier, with Southern hounds contributing to the breed's ancestry. There may also be links to the bloodhound, as manifested not just by the black and tan coloration frequently associated with the Kerry beagle, but also in terms of its long pendulous ears.

It is unclear why these hounds are called beagles though, because they are not small in size, averaging 23in (58cm) at the shoulder, nor do they appear to have varied significantly in height at any stage in their history. In fact, they are better known in Ireland under their native name, which is pocadan, meaning 'hunting dog'. Originally kept for the purpose of stag hunting, these hounds were subsequently used to hunt hares, as they possess both good pace, stamina and scenting skills. Even so, it is not common for them to catch their quarry, with the accompanying hunt master often calling them off before this stage is reached.

During the 1800s, the numbers of Kerry beagles had fallen significantly in Ireland, to the extent that only one major kennel, kept by the Ryan family at Scarteen in County Limerick, still existed. Some of these hounds were taken to America by the Irish settlers however, and in turn played a part in the development of various coonhound breeds there. Today, the numbers of Kerry beagles in Ireland have increased again, although they are a rare sight outside their homeland, and still kept for working rather than exhibition purposes.

Trials involving drag hunting are regularly held, with these hounds revealing that they have picked up the scent by baying loudly. There have

Hunting periods vary, and hounds are often required to hunt in the winter-time, as shown by this treeing Walker coonhound.

Irish wolfhound. A majestic giant among hounds, which almost became extinct during the 19th century.

been no attempts to standardise the breed for show purposes, which helps to explain why although the black and tan form is common, a whole host of other colours including tricolours, tan and white and blue mottled and tan combinations may be seen on occasions in the case of the Kerry beagle.

Ireland is also the home of the largest breed of hound in the world, which is the Irish wolfhound. It can stand up to 35in (90cm) in height, with bitches being slightly shorter than dogs. The Irish wolfhound is a breed of ancient lineage, whose origins date back to antiquity, and its arrival in Ireland has been obscured by the mists of time. It is believed that its ancestors were brought there by the Celts when they invaded this part of western Europe around the second century BC. At this stage in history, large powerful dogs capable of overpowering wolves were important, especially in a country where not only wolves but also other large and dangerous quarry such as wild boar and Irish elk were numerous.

Early descriptions refer to the forerunner of the Irish wolfhound called Cu, with its rough coat and brave nature, coupled with its loyal disposition around the home. Ownership of these dogs was restricted to the nobility for many years and there are many folk tales of individual wolfhounds recorded in Irish history.

Cormac, King of Ireland during the 4th century, owned a famous bitch christened Bran, who was kidnapped and had to be rescued before she could be smuggled to England. It appears that there was a long-standing established trade in Irish wolfhounds, certainly by the 5th century, and probably earlier, with these hounds being dispatched all over Europe.

As history progresses, so it appears that these gigantic hounds were pitched increasingly against wolves rather than other creatures. Indeed in 1652, Oliver Cromwell outlawed their export from the British Isles, considering them to be too valuable for this task. Perhaps ironically, this marked the start of a major period of decline in the wolfhound's history, which almost resulted in its extinction.

The grey wolf was finally eliminated from Ireland by 1800, at a later stage in history than in Britain itself. The Irish wolfhound with its quarry gone then in turn fell dramatically in numbers. Large dogs were expensive to keep, and its homeland was wracked by a series of famines during the 1840s, when human, let alone canine survival was very difficult. Even worse, the ban imposed by Oliver Cromwell remained in force, so that sending stock overseas was impossible.

There were still enthusiasts for the breed however, and the momentum to save these giants from extinction began thanks to the writings of R.D. Richardson at this stage. He owned an Irish wolfhound called Bran, who was to play a significant role in the breed's survival. Others involved during the second half of the 1800s included Sir John Power, and a Scottish army captain called George A. Graham, whose contribution was undoubtedly the greatest of all. He sought out stock that survived, including the hounds from Richardson's kennel, and carried out judicious crosses involving deerhounds, as well as some further outcrosses involving borzois and Great Danes, with the latter in particular serving to increase the size of the remaining wolfhound stock.

The establishment of a breed club in 1895 gave Graham's project greater momentum and recognition in Britain from the Kennel Club was achieved two years later. This marked a major step forward as well, since a definitive standard was established. Up until this time, there had been considerable debate as to what constituted the true Irish wolfhound.

Today, the breed is well known internationally, being taken to the USA at the end of the 19th century. Here in turn it has been crossed again with the Scottish deerhound, to create a further fast-running type of hound, which is sometimes referred to as the American staghound. It appears that this type of breeding is undergoing a renaissance at present, given the availability of stock for outcrossing purposes.

Meanwhile, the Irish wolfhound has developed into a highly affectionate companion and exhibition breed. Although their size may appear intimidating, Irish wolfhounds are more likely to lick an intruder to death rather than savage him or her! Their deep bark is likely to be off-putting however. This is a breed which matures relatively slowly and it will take at least 18 months before a puppy is fully grown. Protracted exercise should not be encouraged during this period, to prevent skeletal damage, although regular exercise is nevertheless vital, as is plenty of space, particularly if these hounds are to live in the home. A brush with the powerful tail of a wolfhound will be sufficient to dispatch cups or ornaments on a low table to the floor.

When seen in profile, the similarity of the Irish wolfhound to the greyhound is apparent, particularly in terms of hind limb structure. The thighs are long and powerful, while the hocks are well let down. The small ears are also reminiscent of a link with the ancestral Southern hound lineage. The coloration of the breed can be varied extending from white through fawn to grey, brindle and black with the same range of colours seen in deerhound being recognised for show purposes. Greys and fawns often predominate today. Sadly however, as one of the giant breeds, the lifespan of the Irish wolfhound tends to be shorter than that of many members of the hound group, with probably ten years or so being an average figure today.

The bloodhound is a breed whose ancestry extends back almost as far as that of the Irish wolfhound. It is still called the St Hubert hound in parts of mainland Europe, commemorating its links to its monastic origins in Belgium (see page 37). It is the only breed of hound which has emerged in the Low Countries. Brought to Britain around the time of the Norman Conquest in 1066, it has contributed to the development of a number of native hound breeds, not least the foxhound. Crosses also took place with Southern hounds and Talbot hounds during the course of its development. Although the name 'bloodhound' may suggest an aggressive disposition, these scenthounds are actually very friendly by nature. Their name probably stems from their aristocratic links, possibly reflecting their pure bred status, in terms of bloodline. Alternatively, it may refer to their abilities to track injured animals or even people, following a trail of tiny drops of blood.

Bloodhounds are well adapted for their task, with large, broad nostrils and pronounced flews which hang down and help to trap scent molecules in the mouth. These will register via Jacobsen's organ in the roof, with this so-called vomeronasal organ connecting directly to the part of the brain involved with smell.

The scenting abilities of bloodhounds are legendary, and although they have been used to hunt escaped prisoners, they have also saved many lives, helping to locate lost children. It has been said that the bloodhound's sense of smell is roughly two million times more sensitive than our own. One of the most famous of all bloodhounds, called Nick Carter, is said to have trailed a criminal following a trail made nearly four and a half days beforehand. During his working lifetime, this single hound tracked down over 600 fugitives.

The scenting skills of the bloodhound are unrivalled. It is a cold-trailing breed, able to follow old scents.

Bloodhounds used to be kept for hunting purposes, but it was not long before their style of hunting was considered too slow. After St Hubert himself died in 727, his pack of St Hubert hounds was moved to the Abbey of Andin, located in the Ardennes. Here they remained, although Charles IX preferred white hounds for hunting purposes and from 1570 onwards, the original forerunners of the bloodhound were kept for tracking purposes, rather than actual hunting.

Even so, there were devotees with packs of bloodhounds, such as Napoleon III (who owned a dozen couples). It appears that the original lineage died out during the French Revolution of 1789, but by that era the breed was also well established overseas, in Britain and elsewhere. The bloodhound has had a major impact on the development of other breeds of hound around the world, with most scenthounds tracing their ancestry back in part to these attractive dogs. Walt Disney's famous cartoon character *Pluto* is also based on the bloodhound.

The typical coloration associated with the breed today is black and tan, with the black forming a saddle over the back extending up to the neck. Other colours include tawny (red), red and tan, and liver and tan. White markings are generally disallowed, aside from small areas on the chest, feet and tip of the tail.

The wrinkled skin on the head of bloodhounds, which contributes to their rather doleful appearance, can be a problem on occasions if the furrows are in close contact, allowing localised skin infections to develop here. Similarly, the exposed inner haws normally hidden in most breeds can become irritated by dust or small pieces of debris entering this area under the eyelid, although breeders are now seeking to prevent these problems arising in the future by selecting away from the most extreme examples.

The basset hound bears a striking resemblance to the bloodhound, in terms of its facial

The basset hound is the best-known representative of its group today. It is a strong, short-legged breed.

appearance, although this breed is very different with regard to the rest of its physique. The description 'basset' originates from the French word *bas* meaning low, which describes the height of these hounds. Although developed in Britain, the origin of the basset hound, as with other bassets, lies in France, but it has established a stronger international following at present than other similar breeds.

Bassets were first described in the latter part of the 16th century. In his book *La Venérie*, the author de Fouilloux describes hounds with short, crooked legs that were being kept in the province of Artois. They may have been derived from St Hubert hounds, afflicted by a mutation which had resulted in this reduction in stature. Such dogs were soon popular for hunting purposes, as they could be accompanied on foot. This style of hunting increased rapidly in popularity after the French Revolution of 1789, when the traditional style of aristocratic hunting, with riders on horseback, had been condemned and many packs of larger hounds were wiped out.

The basset hound itself is closely related to the breed known today as the basset Artésian Normand, which was developed by the bloodhound enthusiast, the Comte le Coultreux de Canteleu. It was first exhibited publicly in 1863 in Paris, at the first organised dog show held in the city. Three years later, Lord Galway received the first examples of the breed to be seen in Britain, called Basset and Belle. Some of their progeny were passed to Lord Onslow, who sought further examples of the breed from the count's pack in Normandy.

Sir John Everett Millais was also among those instrumental in promoting the development of the basset hound in Britain. His stud dog called Model caused a sensation when entered at a Wolverhampton dog show in 1873. By pairings of the basset Artésian Normand with beagle and bloodhound stock, Sir John laid the foundations for the contemporary basset hound, carrying out the first successful recorded case of canine artificial insemination to achieve this aim, necessitated by the difference in height between basset and bloodhound.

The lasting influence of the latter is clearly apparent even today, as shown by the heavily wrinkled skin of the forehead, longer head and more pronounced ears than the basset Artésian Normand. The basset hound was officially recognised by the Kennel Club in Britain in 1880, while its French relative remains scarce there. A breed club was established four years later, and unusually in this case, basset hounds started to be used for hunting purposes after they made their entry into the show ring. The Wolverhampton pack was the first to be established in 1891.

Basset hounds have subsequently also built up a strong following in North America for their hunting prowess, often participating in field trials organised by the American Kennel Club. There is a clear divergence in type often apparent between basset hounds kept for hunting purposes and those bred for the show ring, whose features tend to be more exaggerated. Hunting bassets tend to have straighter legs and less pronounced folds of skin on their bodies, bearing a closer resemblance to their Artésian Normand ancestor.

Perhaps not surprisingly however, the unusual appearance of the basset hound has led to these dogs attracting considerable publicity over recent years, thanks to the long running Fred Basset cartoon strip by Graham and their association with snug-fitting shoes, which in turn has helped to encourage their popularity as household companions.

Active and inquisitive by nature, these hounds show the typical attributes of their larger relatives. While proving friendly and affectionate they also possess quite a loud bark, suggestive to would-be

Basset hounds are not fleet of foot, but they are exceedingly determined when working as a pack following a scent.

intruders of a much larger dog. The food intake of basset hounds needs to be strictly regulated to prevent obesity which can place serious strains on their short legs, especially as they will instinctively prove to be gluttonous if given the opportunity.

Behind the basset's solemn demeanour, there lurks an iron will, which can make training difficult. What may have been learnt in the confines of a garden is often immediately ignored once an interesting scent beckons in the wider world, while catching up with a rampaging basset is not always as simple as may be thought, especially across rough terrain, where bushes are numerous. Tricolours are probably the most common colour variant, although lemon and white, or indeed any hound colour, is acceptable for show purposes.

The development of the basset Artésian Normand in the latter half of the 19th century also occurred on separate lines. Those bred by the Comte le Coultreux de Canteleu were evolved essentially for hunting purposes, with stamina and straight, albeit short legs being essential attributes of the breed. Their facial features were regarded as being similar to those of the chien d'Artois, which probably played a role in their development, as exemplified by their relatively small ears.

The original Artois bassets were invariably bicoloured, which enabled them to be distinguished from their tricoloured Normand relatives. Another breeder, M. Louis Lane, who lived near Rouen, was developing a more elaborate strain, compared with that of the Comte, stressing the aesthetic appeal of the noble head and longer ears. Unfortunately, the legs of M. Lane's bassets were far less straight, and notably shorter, resulting in some individuals being badly handicapped.

It was left to M. Léon Verrier, who also resided near Rouen, to fuse the characteristics of both strains together successfully. His efforts led to the formation of a breed society in 1910 and the merger of the Artois (Artésian) and Normand

Basset Artésian Normand. This breed can be easily distinguished from the basset hound since its skull is less domed, and its legs are straighter.

strains led to these bassets being rechristened as the basset Artésian Normand, which is often abbreviated, particularly in their homeland, to BAN. Keen and lively by nature, packs of these bassets are regularly used especially in northern France for hunting rabbits and hares, particularly in areas which are heavily wooded and so inaccessible to larger hounds.

In terms of coloration, these bassets are almost invariably tricoloured, with black dominating over the body while the extremities are white, offset against rich tan coloration elsewhere. Bicolours are now very scarce and rarely seen, while on occasions a red individual crops up, although these also are not popular. An unusual feature associated with this breed is the presence of a distinctive curl of hair over each hip joint in many cases.

The chien d'Artois, which played an important part in the development of the basset Artésian Normand is an ancient breed, first recorded in the vicinity of northern France during the 15th century. It may even have had a role in the development of the beagle. Unfortunately, the subsequent importation of British breeds to this part of France in the 19th century resulted in cross-breeding, as did matings with a taller hound found in this region, called the Normand, which has since become extinct.

The future of the chien d'Artois itself hung very much in the balance by the 1880s when two enthusiasts called Ernest Levair and M. Therouanne set out to resurrect this ancient breed. Their attempts were successful, until the Great War intervened, throwing the future of this breed again into uncertainty.

A more recent breeding programme begun during the 1970s has since resulted in the re-emergence of the chien d'Artois, which is characterised by its large, heavy head, long, broad ears and tricoloured patterning. This breed is also simply known as the briquet, reflecting the crosses with gun dogs that took place during the 1890s, with this name translating as 'small braque'.

The links existing between English and French hounds are most obviously reflected in the Anglo-French group of breeds. The largest member of this category is the grand Anglo-Français which can stand up to 27in (68.5cm) tall. It was bred by crossings between larger French hounds and foxhounds, with the name of the ancestral French hound being included for a period in their early history, such as Anglo-Français – Poitevin. The prefix of bâtard was often used as well, to indicate their cross-bred ancestry.

Standardisation began in earnest in 1957, when these hounds became categorised under their current general heading of grand Anglo-Français, divided into three categories on the basis of their coloration. The tricolore is the most widely kept example of this group and reflects its foxhound ancestry not just in its coloration, but also in the shape of its head, which is less refined than that of the Poitevin itself. Their large size enables these hounds to be used for hunting large quarry, including wild boar and deer.

Less well known is the grand Anglo-Français blanc et noir, which is descended from Gascon-Saintongeois and bleu de Gascogne stock. This is not only reflected in part by their coloration, but also in their heavily boned appearance. Black and white coloration predominates although there is a hint of the tricoloured appearance of the foxhound notably by small pale yellow areas on the face. The development of the grand Anglo-Français hounds began at the end of the 19th century, but the third member of the group, known as the blanc et orange, bred from Billy stock, remains by far the rarest. Breeders have been aiming to establish a type approximating to the tricolore, with the use of crosses involving the Billy and lemon and white foxhounds. As a result, it has not proved easy to establish the required type.

Apart from their size it is possible to distinguish between the grand and two other sizes of Anglo-French hound by virtue of their relatively small ears and stockier bodies. The middle sized hounds in the family are described simply as the Français or the Anglo-Français de moyen vénerie group. They stand approximately 20in (50cm) tall and exist in the same range of colours as their larger relatives, although again, the blanc et orange remains scarce. While some of these Français hounds are kept as household companions, they do retain strong hunting instincts and need plenty of exercise when living in such surroundings. They are not well known at present outside France.

The smaller of the Anglo-French hounds is the Anglo-Français de petite vénerie group, created by crossings between beagles or beagle harriers and medium-sized, smooth-coated French breeds including the Poitevin and porcelaine. Their height is quite varied falling within the range of 18–21in (46–53cm), while their ancestry means they more closely resemble the Poitevin rather than being a smaller version of the grand Anglo-Français.

They are keen hunters of hares and rabbits, working in packs, but they are not well standardised as yet for show purposes. Tricoloured individuals are most common but both black and white and orange and white varieties are encountered on occasions. A survey carried out in France in 1992 revealed that the Anglo-Français de petite vénerie is nevertheless one of the more popular of this family of hounds with nearly 400 individuals being recorded. They are also rising in popularity as pets, proving both affectionate and active by nature.

The foxhound has also played a part in the survival of other French breeds however, especially after the French Revolution of 1789 when a number of the ancient breeds became extinct or were seriously decimated in numbers. The Poitevin managed to survive this traumatic period in history, but only just, with the owner of the most highly regarded of the three bloodlines, called M. Larye, having been guillotined. This pack had originally been created by his family back in 1692, as the result of six couples of foxhounds from the Dauphin. These hounds were crossed with others in that area of Haut-Poitou in the west of France, and soon established an unrivalled reputation for hunting wolves.

The large strain was distinguished not only on the grounds of its physical prowess, but also its tricoloured appearance. Their stamina was renowned, with their voice serving to keep the accompanying huntsmen in touch with the progress of the hounds. Two other strains of the chien de Haut-Poitou (as these hounds were known until 1957) were also developed from the staghounds of the region, being described as the Céris and Montemboeuf after their creators. They were generally not as highly regarded as the Larye hounds however, and instantly distinguishable by their bicoloured appearance.

After the Revolution, the brothers de la Besage of Montmorillon, who lived in Poitou, sought to revive the breed, but with only two of the Larye hounds still known to be alive, this posed a formidable challenge. Their endeavours were proving successful however, when a cruel twist of fate once more threw the breed's future into doubt. Their kennels were decimated by an attack of rabies in 1842, and necessitated the importation of foxhounds from England two years later, to save the breed at this stage. By careful selection for type however, the influence of the foxhound has dramatically waned over the course of three generations, with regard to key features such as the length of the Poitevin ears, which are traditionally longer and narrower in appearance.

Further crossings involving foxhounds were necessary to reconstitute this ancient breed after the end of the Second World War. Packs of these athletic hounds are now kept for hunting deer and wild boar, often capable of running for over seven hours, at an average speed of 5mph (8kph). Although not especially shy, the Poitevin is rather less friendly by nature than many scenthounds and thrives only in the security of a pack. Tricolours still predominate today although occasional bicolours do crop up.

The Billy bears a close relationship to the Poitevin, showing a common ancestry. The breed was created by M. Hublot de Rivault who resided at the Château de Billy in Poitou. He established a pack of chiens de Haut-Poitou in 1877 at a time before foxhound crossings had occurred to any significant extent, so that his hounds represented an extension of the original lineages. M. Hublot de Rivault was drawn to the paler coloration associated with the Montemboeuf and Céris strains however, and ultimately coloration became the main feature when selecting stock for breeding purposes. Billys were bred in white, lemon and white or a pale *café au lait* shade and white. Almost certainly, the Billy represents the lineage which extends back to the grand chien blanc de roi which were kept by the kings of France as staghounds (see page 48).

The pack developed at Château de Billy was

dispersed in 1927, with their creator dying nine years later. This could have marked the end of the breed, but after the Second World War, de Rivault's son Anthony set out on a quest to recreate the Billy. He was able to obtain a couple of these hounds, called Volga and Vol-au-Vent, using these as the basis for his breeding programme.

Judicious use of crosses involving Poitevins as well as the pale coloured porcelaine and harriers, saw his ambition realised, before his death in 1975. Even so, these attractively coloured hounds are still quite rare in France today, although various packs are now established. Roe deer are their usual quarry, although two packs in recent times have been used regularly for hunting wild boar, which prove a far more formidable adversary.

The Billy's ears sit relatively high on the skull and lie quite flat, in contrast to most French breeds. This is thought to be a legacy of the harrier blood used in its recreation. In contrast to the Poitevin of today, the Billy also has a shorter, more rounded skull and a bigger muzzle, often with signs of a dewlap not associated with its relative.

Aside from the Billy, one of the most distinctively coloured of the large French hounds is the grand bleu de Gascogne, whose origins lie in the arid south-west region of the country. It is a very old breed, linked with the old Southern hound of England, which is not so surprising, given that this region of France was under English rule for 380 years from 1150 onwards. The grand bleu de Gascogne was kept by Gaston Phoebus (see page 44), and also Henry IV of France (1553–1610).

Grand bleu de Gascogne. Its blue coloration stems from the mottling created by the white and black hairs.

It was introduced to the New World as early as the 17th century, and built up a strong following there. George Washington was presented with a pack of seven of these hounds by General Lafayette in 1785 and subsequently recorded that soon afterwards, one of these bitches produced a litter of fifteen puppies. He also compared their melodious voices with the bells of Moscow! The legacy of these early imports is to be seen in various native American hounds, notably the blue tick coonhound (see page 143), and there are now reputedly more grands bleus de Gascogne in the USA than France.

Their appearance has changed somewhat down the years however, with examples of the breed seen a century ago tending to show much greater areas of black than those of today. There is now much greater emphasis on the distinctive dense mottling, resulting from the overlay of black and white hairs which result in the impression of the characteristic blue coloration. It is thought that this mottling may help to give some protection against the sun when these hounds are working in their homeland. Clear white areas of any size are not favoured. Tan markings are present above the eyes however, with similar coloration on the muzzle and tan mottling also evident on the limbs.

The grand bleu de Gascogne is the largest member of the group. It shows more mottling today than in the past.

The chestnut coloured patch over each eye is a characteristic seen in all forms of the bleu de Gascogne.

The grand bleu de Gascogne used to be kept for hunting wolves in the past, with this activity being captured by the artist Jules Gelibert in a famous work painted in 1884, portraying a pack owned by Baron de Ruble. In the field, this breed is a relatively slow and ponderous worker, and so is kept essentially for hunting hares rather than large quarry. It is a highly talented tracker with a calm, friendly nature and requires plenty of exercise.

As is often the case with French hounds, smaller forms of the grand bleu de Gascogne have been developed, as well as a rough coated griffon variety. The petit bleu de Gascogne stands at least 20in (50cm) in height, which is roughly 4in (10cm) shorter than its larger relative. It was bred directly from the grand bleu de Gascogne with the smallest individuals being selected for this purpose. Its principal quarry is rabbits and hares. The ears in this case are less curled and thicker, while the head is often finer in appearance. Perhaps strangely, this smaller variety is almost unknown outside the south-west of France.

The basset form is the smallest member of the bleu de Gascogne grouping, typically standing between 13–16in (34–42cm) tall. Although this breed existed in the past, it had effectively died out by 1911, when M. Alan Bourbon sought examples in the Midi where it had been kept and used for hunting purposes previously. He then set out to create the breed, using basset Saintongeois stock, having located just three examples of these similarly mottled hounds. The breeding programme also entailed the use of larger bleu de Gascogne hounds, with the resulting puppies becoming shorter in stature over several generations, until the basset height was achieved. After the First World War some crossings with bassets Artésian Normand took place.

Basset bleu de Gascogne. A short-legged version of the grand, but with the same distinctive appearance.

Few other hound breeders appear to have shared M. Bourbon's enthusiasm for this breed in the past and only relatively recently have the numbers of the basset bleu de Gascogne started to increase to any appreciable extent. Their attractive coloration has played a part in this revival, as has an improvement in soundness, which has made them more suitable for working purposes as pack hounds. Like their larger relatives, they have very keen scenting skills and an attractive voice, but lack pace in comparison with other bassets.

The petit griffon de Gascogne has a basically identical coloration to that of the petit bleu de Gascogne, but is instantly recognisable by its longer, rough coat, which must not have a woolly texture. The griffon is also slightly shorter than the smooth coated petit form from which it was derived by crossings with French griffons. The distinctive eyebrows of longer hair transposed into the petit griffon bleu de Gascogne are a notable feature, and must not obscure the eyes. A standard was first established for it in 1919. Although regarded as the rarest of the native hound breeds of France in recent years, the signs are that this member of the Gascogne group is now more firmly established again. Fifty-five individuals were recorded in a survey carried out in 1991, with the breed attracting greatest support in the south-west of the country.

A very similar breed to the grand bleu de Gascogne also occurs in this region of France, taking its name in part from the old province of Saintonge, adjoining Gascogne. Although sadly the Saintongeois hound itself is now extinct, having plummeted in numbers as a result of the French Revolution which only three individuals – two dogs and a bitch – survived, the influence of the breed lives on through the grand Gascon-Saintongeois.

The three Saintongeois hounds left alive ultimately passed into the care of Baron de Carayon-la-Tour. He sought to maintain the lineage by using crossings involving the grand bleu de Gascogne, from the leading kennel of Baron de Ruble. The resulting puppies were divided between the two men on the basis of their coloration, which was either mottled or solid in colour. The breeding programme continued for some time, but ultimately the two lines merged, with the breed then becoming known under its present name.

The Saintongeois legacy is apparent in the finer head shape and muzzle of these hounds, compared with the grand bleu de Gascogne itself. They also have more pace, but retain the determined nature of the grand bleu de Gascogne on the trail and probably match this breed's scenting abilities.

Further refinement of the grand Gascon-Saintongeois carried out by M. Rogatien Levesque, begun during 1813 in Brittany, led to the development of the Levesque breed named after its creator. Unfortunately it has now disappeared. Such hounds were characterised by the prominent area of black often likened to a blanket covering the entire back and the lack of any ticking. In contrast the grand Gascon-Saintongeois has black areas mainly restricted to the head, with ticking and often some black patches apparent elsewhere and is heavier overall than its extinct relative. It is thought that the last remaining examples of the Levesque became grouped into the breeding programme for the grand Anglo-Français blanc et noir when standardisation occurred during 1957.

The grand Gascon-Saintongeois is used for hunting a variety of larger game, including deer and wild boar. There is now also a smaller version of this breed, known as the petit Gascon-Saintongeois, which is roughly 3in or so (7.5cm) shorter in stature. Its principal quarry is hares and rabbits. A characteristic greyish coloured area is normally present above the hock in both cases. This is described as the *marque de chevreuil*, meaning 'mark of the deer'.

The Gascon-Saintongeois and the bleu de Gascogne have been used together, along with chien d'Artois blood, to create the Ariègeois, which is a relative newcomer on the French hound scene. Local medium-sized 'briquet' hounds also played a part in its development as might be expected from their ancestry. The Ariègeois has a mottled appearance to an extent, although black and white areas predominate on the coat. Pale tan markings are confined to the area above the eyes and in the vicinity of the jowls.

The homeland of this breed is in the far south of France in the province of Ariège, adjoining the border with Spain. The terrain is hilly and hunting opportunities are limited. The Ariègeois's usual quarry is hares, which it uses its keen sense of smell to track. First recognised by the Club Gaston Phoebus in 1907, this breed became very scarce after the Second World War, but has undergone something of a revival since the late 1970s. An unusual feature associated with the Ariègeois is that on rare occasions, totally black puppies may crop up in their litters.

The elegant porcelaine hound originates from the south-east of the country, close to the border with Switzerland, in the province of Franche-Comte. These hounds are of ancient lineage, being descended from the grand chien blanc du roi (see page 48). As with many French hounds, this breed was called chien de Franche-Comte at first, after the area where it originated, before its name was changed to reflect its appearance. The porcelaine is almost entirely white, apart from some orange spots on its body, notably its ears.

Just prior to the French Revolution, many of these particular hounds were taken abroad by their aristocratic owners, notably to the United States. The Rousseau family, who owned a large part of Louisiana Territory, thanks to a generous gift from Louis XIV, had perhaps the largest collection of these hounds. Prior to the American Civil War of 1861–5, their pack was comprised of some 250 individuals. One famous portrait from this era shows a group overcoming a puma (*Felis concolor*) in a cane field. Ironically however, revolutionary fervour finally destroyed this pack in their adopted homeland, with the survivors of the Rousseaus being force to head west into Texas, taking their surviving hounds with them, which ultimately became dispersed through the region and incorporated into the developing lineages of native American hounds.

The porcelaine effectively died out in Europe as a result of the French Revolution, but was revived as a breed thanks to careful use of the Swiss Schweizer laufhund stock during the first half of the 19th century. Modern bloodlines all stem from the hounds donated by the last Abbot of Luxeuil, M. de Clermont-Tonnere to his physician Dr Poillot, who lived in Montbazon. A couple of these hounds in turn were acquired by the Marquis de Foudras, who established a famous pack from them which hunted in the south-west of France for over 30 years up until 1896.

The Marquis introduced both Billy and West Country harrier stock to improve the vigour of his developing pack, and this also had the effect of improving the pace of the resulting hounds. Today's porcelaine is a smaller, lighter dog than its pre-revolution ancestor. The slightly glossy white coat, conveying the appearance of fine porcelain has been effectively retained however, and is one of the reasons underlying the breed's popularity today. The skin under the fine hair may be mottled, creating a bluish glaze on the coat itself. Packs of these hounds are quite widely kept, not just in France but also in other neighbouring parts of Europe including Switzerland and Italy. Hares are their principal quarry.

It is not only smooth-coated hounds which have found favour in France however, as reflected by the various griffon breeds. This name is derived from a clerk employed by the French royal family in the 15th century, who bred such hounds. He was known under his job title of *greffier*, which ultimately became modified to 'griffon' to describe these wire-coated hounds. The most popular group today are the griffons Vendéen, whose origins lie in the La Vendée district which is located south of Brittany, on France's west coast.

The grand griffon Vendéen is the largest member of the four breeds, standing at least 24in (61cm) tall. These griffons were originally kept for hunting wolves in packs, being courageous by nature, although also possessing a strong independent streak in their make-up. They are thought to be the result of cross-breeding between rough-coated and now extinct French breeds such as the Auvergne or Bresse and the smooth-coated chiens du Poitou. Their numbers were again badly affected by the French

Grand basset griffon Vendéen. One of four distinctive varieties of wire-coated hound, created in the Vendée region of France.

Revolution, while subsequently the smaller members of the group were considered more suitable for hunting purposes, but especially in recent years, the popularity of the grand griffon Vendéen has grown again.

Lighter coloured individuals are preferred, such as fawn, but bicolours are also often seen. These hounds are now usually pitched against wild boar, with their tousled coats giving them good protection when hunting in the dense undergrowth often encountered in their native region. The future of the grand griffon Vendéen is now relatively secure, with packs also being established overseas, most notably in the USA.

The briquet griffon Vendéen is typically about 4in (10cm) shorter in height at the shoulder than the grand form, with the word 'briquet' meaning 'hare hunting'. Although kept in small packs comprised of two or three couples, these hounds are also sometimes worked individually, when with better control, their enthusiasm can be more effectively channelled, since they do have a reputation for being too eager in the field. The head of the briquet griffon Vendéen is not as long as the other members of the group, and so may not appear as balanced as a result.

The griffons Vendéen are unique amongst French hounds in occurring in four different height categories, thanks to two basset forms. The grand basset griffon Vendéen is approximately 2in (5cm) taller on average than its petit relative. One of the most famous of all lines was maintained by the Desamy family for over a century, at La Chaize-le-Vicomte in the Vendée. Their grand bassets were so well standardised at 42cm

The long ears of the grand basset griffon Vendéen hang forward either side of the nose when these scenthounds are on a trail.

The coat of the fauve de Bretagne has a decidedly coarse, hard texture, with a distinctive coloration.

(16.5in) that these hounds were identified throughout France as the '42 Desamys'. Tricoloured individuals are much more common in this case, although fawns are not actively encouraged. More definite coat contrasts, such as black and white are favoured in the basset breeds, compared with their larger relatives. The coat itself has a harsh texture, with any woolly feel being viewed as a serious flaw. The legs in all cases are straight and must not be crooked.

The petit basset griffon Vendéen is even more popular than the grand form, and ranks as one of the most widely kept of all French breeds, having established a very large following in its homeland. As with other bassets however, some individuals may suffer from inter-vertebral disc weakness on occasions, but otherwise they make lively, enjoyable companions, being full of character. These bassets can also hunt effectively with packs pursuing hares and rabbits.

The basset fauve de Bretagne is even smaller than the petit basset griffon Vendéen, being recognised as the shortest of all French breeds, standing as short as 13in (32cm). It was bred from crosses between the larger griffon fauve de Bretagne in the region of Brittany where both breeds developed, and the basset griffon Vendéen. There was a time when the future of this solid-coloured basset was in doubt, but further crosses with the Vendéen bassets and possibly red wire-haired dachshunds ensured its survival. The coat of the basset fauve de Bretagne is different from that of the Vendée breeds, being hard and close.

Clearer evidence for the influence of the dachshund may be evident in the gait of the basset fauve de Bretagne, which is something of a swagger. Their coloration can vary in depth from a pale shade of wheaten through to red, with some individuals having a small white area on the chest.

The petit basset griffon Vendéen, dubbed the PBGV, is the most widely kept member of the group.

The popularity of the basset fauve de Bretagne has grown significantly over recent years, and not just in France. These lively little hounds are not the most responsive to training however, being very strong-willed by nature. They are traditionally hunted as two couples, but increasingly they are being used on their own in this respect. Plenty of exercise is essential for them.

The larger form, known as the griffon fauve de Bretagne, has a very long history dating back to medieval times, being especially valued for hunting the wolves which then plagued the region. A pack was kept by François I (1515–47) and the breed retained close links with royalty over the centuries, being described in 1570 by King Charles IX, but by the mid-19th century these hounds effectively no longer existed in a pure state. Attempts to revive the breed were then undertaken in the 1880s, using the briquet griffon Vendéen and proved successful.

The griffon fauve de Bretagne is now bred in the same colour range as the basset form, with a medium length, hard textured coat. Its continued existence is due to the efforts of M. de Lamandé who managed to maintain 12 of these hounds in his kennels, which were vital for its revival. The breed has grown in popularity since the end of the Second World War.

Griffon fauve de Bretagne. This breed was originally used for wolf-hunting, but has since proved an adaptable gundog.

The griffon Nivernais is another ancient French breed which could share a common ancestry with the griffon fauve de Bretagne. They were bred from grand griffon Vendéen stock, which had established a formidable reputation as wolf hunters. One pack of 13 individuals accounted for more than 200 wolves at the start of the 19th century in the area of Morvan. These hounds were ultimately crossed with other local hounds in the region including a noted foxhound called Archer. The resulting cross-bred hounds ultimately became known as griffons Vendéen Nivernais, and finally once the Vendéen influence had disappeared, the breed was recognised as the griffon Nivernais.

It has a longer body and is typically greyish in colour, with light shades, tricolours or black individuals not being favoured. In this respect, they most closely resemble the extinct gris de St Louis breed which used to be kept in this wooded part of France. These hounds have a bold, fearless nature. They are now kept for hunting wild boar especially in their homeland of the Nivernais, working typically in packs of two or two and a half couples. Unlike other griffon breeds, which can be rather excitable, the griffon Nivernais has a reputation for being quite phlegmatic.

Chapter 6
The Hounds of Eastern Europe, Asia and Australia

Being bred essentially for hunting purposes, hounds have been evolved to match the terrain in which they are expected to work, as well as their quarry. This is perhaps most apparent in the case of the dachshund breeds, which are of German origin. Their Anglicised name actually translates as 'badger dog' indicating their traditional opponent. The hunting style of the dachshund is such that it could be considered a terrier however, rather than a true hound, because these dogs actually battle with the badger underground in its sett, rather than pursuing it over any distance. Part of the confusion may have originated from the incorporation of the word 'hund' into its name, which may be suggestive of the term 'hound', but actually means 'dog'.

In spite of their short-legged appearance, there is no official height standard laid down for either the standard or miniature varieties, but they are typically within a range of 5–10in (13–25cm). In fact, the only measurement traditionally associated with the dachshund is the circumference of its chest, a key dimension for a hound which ventures into underground tunnels. In Germany, where the breed is known as the teckel, working dachshunds are still classified in this way. The standard form, called the normalschlag, should have a chest measurement of over 14in (35cm), with that of the miniature or zwergteckel being in the range of 12–14in (31–35cm). There is also a third category in Germany, the kaninchenteckel, kept for rabbit hunting, which has a chest circumference of less than 12in (31cm).

Although not fast above ground, dachshunds can prove talented trackers when required, thus revealing a decidedly hound-like aspect to their nature. They are also very brave dogs, with badgers proving to be formidable adversaries, particularly underground where there is no escape from their teeth and ferocious claws. The origins of the dachshund remain something of a mystery however, although woodcuts suggest that these small dogs were already in existence by the 16th century.

Similar images have been recorded from ancient Egypt and Mexico, which has led to suggestions that such dogs could have been the ancestors of today's dachshunds. It seems far more likely however, that the breed is of much more recent origin, stemming from a similar mutation that cropped up in Europe, resulting in

Smooth-coated dachshund. One of three coat types associated with this popular breed.

a shortening of the limbs. Such genetic occurrences are not uncommon in domestic livestock, ranging from Dexter cattle to the feline parallel of the dachshund, which is called the munchkin. Such cats have bodies of normal size, but dramatically shortened legs. The facial features of the dachshund are certainly not dissimilar to those of other taller breeds of German origin.

The original form was the smooth-haired standard dachshund, sometimes rather derogatorily described as the 'sausage dog', a nickname that appears to have arisen in Britain during the First World War when opposition to Germany was at its height. In the early days, it was not that uncommon for these hounds to have white markings in their coats, which is also rather suggestive of a large hound ancestry. Although it is sometimes proposed that French bassets could have been involved in their development, this seems unlikely since the dachshund would appear to pre-date the likely candidates in this field.

Dachshunds are unusual in being classified on the basis of their chest measurements.

A miniature smooth-haired dachshund. This is, in effect, a scaled-down version of the standard form.

The breed was first introduced to Britain during the 1840s when Albert, the Prince Consort, was given some from the kennels of Prince Edward of Saxe-Weinar. They were kept at the royal residence at Windsor just outside London, and participated at pheasant shoots, presumably helping to drive the birds towards the waiting guns.

The popularity of the breed, then called the German badger hound, subsequently rose dramatically and it was often represented at the early dog shows. Between 1876 and 1877, a Mr Schuller alone reputedly imported over 200 dachshunds from Germany, in an attempt to meet the demand. The Dachshund Club was founded on 7 January 1881 in London, with its standard based on the features that were then most apparent in the breed. Significant differences were to emerge in the standard formulated seven years later by the German Dachshund Club however, based on the ancestral type, but it was not until 1907 that the original English standard for the breed was finally superseded.

The British love affair with the breed ended dramatically following the outbreak of the First World War, because of the dachshund's Teutonic links. By the 1920s, when a revival of interest began, the old bloodlines had largely died out in Britain, necessitating the acquisition of further stock from Germany. The smooth-haired dachshund had soon established a keen following, and subsequently was not singled out for criticism during the Second World War as had been the case earlier in the century.

Today, apart from the traditional smooth-coated form, there are both wire-haired and long-haired varieties existing in both the standard and miniature categories. Wire-haired dachshunds were produced as a result of cross-breedings involving various terriers, notably the Dandie Dinmont, while long-hairs were the product of crosses with various gundogs, notably the German stöber. Then on the basis of selecting for

Miniature wire-haired dachshund. The coat is mainly short, and harsh in texture, with the undercoat being softer.

ABOVE AND BELOW: The head of a miniature wire-haired dachshund, showing the smooth ears, bushy eyebrows and the beard.

size, the miniature varieties were evolved. Coat care in these cases is clearly more demanding than for the smooth-coated varieties. The choice of colours available in the case of dachshunds is also extensive, with all but pure white individuals being recognised for show purposes. Even so, reds, brindles and black and tan tend to be most commonly seen, rather than merle or white and yellow combinations.

The popularity of the dachshund in its many forms remains strong throughout the world today, with the town of Gergweis in Germany laying claim to the title of 'Dachshund Capital of the World'. Here there are said to be twice as many of these hounds as people, and this location draws breed enthusiasts from around the globe.

Lively by nature, dachshunds possess a bark well in excess of their size, suggestive of a much larger dog, and they will prove to be alert guardians. Less popular with owners, however is their innate tendency to tunnel, as they will often venture into flower beds for this purpose. They may also be tempted down rabbit and similar burrows when out for a walk, with close supervision being recommended in such surroundings.

Smooth-haired dachshund. The coat is short, sleek and smooth, with the underlying skin being loose.

It is also a good idea to exercise these hounds on a leash and harness rather than a collar, which could damage their rather delicate spinal column. Intervertebral disc protrusions are commonly associated with dachshunds, and they should not be encouraged to clamber up stairs or on to chairs for fear of triggering an injury of this nature.

Dachshunds in turn have contributed to the development of other German breeds, in the form of members of the dachsbracke group, which have evolved not only in Germany but also neighbouring Austria. The Westphalian dachsbracke originated in the areas of Westphalia and the Sauerland, which is why it is sometimes called the Sauerlander dachsbracke in its homeland. These hounds are used for working on an individual basis with their owners rather than as part of a pack in the wooded alpine areas where similar dogs have been kept for hundreds of years.

The Westphalian dachsbracke was first named in 1886, and then recognised for show purposes in 1935. The breed is either tricoloured or red and white in colour. It has a loud call, indicating that quarry has been located with certainty, while its short stature, often no more than 12in (31cm) at the shoulder, frequently enables a much closer undetected approach than could be achieved by a larger hound.

The Deutsche bracke is significantly taller, averaging between 16–21in (40–53cm) in height and was developed in the same area of Germany. There used to be a variety of different strains of hound known under distinctive names such as Sauerlander holzbracke and Steinbracke, which was slightly smaller. They prove versatile hunters, especially on a hot trail, pursuing quarry ranging from rabbits and hares to wild boar, with their

ABOVE AND BELOW: Deutsche bracke. These hounds have been evolved to work in wooded countryside.

melodic voices echoing across the wooded valleys. It was also not unknown for them to be trained as retrievers.

Finally, these various forms which shared a common ancestry were then grouped together, with a standard being agreed during 1955. The Deutsche bracke today is tricoloured in appearance, with a prominent black saddle. White areas are restricted to the extremities of the body, on the feet and tip of the tail, as well as forming a blaze and neck ring, with white hair also extending to the underparts.

The Alpenlandischer dachsbracke is similar in stature to its Westphalian relative, but in this case white markings of any type are discouraged. Shades of red and black therefore predominate in its coat, which has a relatively coarse texture. Dachshunds again may have contributed to the development of this breed with its legs being short but straight. The Alpine dachsbracke was first recognised in its own right in 1975 although it remains very localised, being essentially unknown outside its home region. The breed is valued primarily for its deer tracking skills, although it can also hunt other game, working in close association with its owner.

The integral links between the hounds of Austria and Germany are also reflected in the case of larger breeds, such as the Bayrischer gebirgs

schweisshund, also known as the Bavarian schweisshund or Bavarian mountain dog. These scenthounds were bred from the heavier Hanoverian hound crossed with lighter Tyrolean hounds, to improve their pace but without compromising their tracking skills in the mountainous region of Bavaria. Here they are highly valued for tracking deer which have been wounded by a hunter, and must be put out of their misery.

The description 'schweisshund' actually means 'bloodhound' and refers to the remarkable ability of these hounds to follow a trail of this type. Their coloration can range from wheaten to red, also brindle and tan, with the facial area being blackish, while the actual appearance of the head is somewhat reminiscent of a dachshund. The Bavarian schweisshund has a reputation for being phlegmatic by nature, and a dedicated worker, although it is virtually unknown outside the region where it was first developed in the early 1900s.

Its Hanoverian ancestor, known as the Hannoverscher schweisshund remains a larger, heavier dog, standing up to 4in (10cm) taller at 24in (61cm). Its coloration is similar. The Hanoverian hound was originally bred during the 19th century, although its ancestry probably dates back to the leithund, which may have fulfilled a similar role in this part of central Europe as long ago as the 5th century. It was a close relative of the St Hubert hound which accounts for its descendant's excellent tracking skills. There is a record of a Hanoverian hound successfully following a trail made over a week previously, for a distance of over 30 miles (48km). In the past these hounds worked in packs, but today they invariably work singly, in the company of their owner, traditionally being used like their Bavarian relative to locate injured game.

The ancestral stock of Celtic brackes, which were known in the Alpine region back in the medieval period, have played a vital part in the development of a number of the breeds seen in the region today. Among these is the Tyroler bracke, also known as the Tyrolean hound. It is named after the area of Austria adjoining the Alps in the west of the country, and occurs in both a standard and miniature form, attaining a maximum height of roughly 19in (48cm). The coat tends to be short, but can be wiry, and is typically black or black and tan, although other colours such as fawn are seen on occasions.

The development of the Tyroler bracke began in earnest during the 1860s, with the breed then being exhibited for the first time in 1896, at a show in Innsbruck. These hounds have proved to be versatile hunting companions, as capable of working a hot trail, pursuing fox or rabbit, or trailing an injured deer. Little known outside their home region, these hounds will form a strong bond with their owners, while remaining essentially as working companions rather than pets.

The Austrian brandlbracke or Österreichischer glat thaariger bracke is a lighter type of hound, with longer legs than its Tyrolean counterpart, although being of a similar height. There are links between this Austrian smooth-haired hound and the Swiss Jura hounds, as well as the Celtic bracke. In terms of coloration, it is either red or black and tan – white areas on the coat are permitted, if restricted to the vicinity of the chest and feet, or in the form of a ring around the neck. A versatile hunting breed, like others from the region, these hounds are kept entirely for this purpose, rather than the show ring, even though they are generally friendly by nature.

The native name of Steirischer rauh-haarige hochgebirgs bracke describes the typical hunting

Austrian brandlbracke. Its name reflects its coloration, with 'brandl' meaning 'little fire', describing its reddish-tan markings.

Typical terrain for the Austrian brandlbracke. These scenthounds are usually quiet when hunting.

Austrian brandlbrackes form a close bond with their owners, working keenly alongside them.

terrain of these hounds, with 'hochgebirgs' meaning 'high mountains'. Their English description of Styrian rough-haired mountain hound is also reflective of their native haunts, with the breed originating in the southern Austrian province of Styria. The breed owes its existence in part to the efforts of an enthusiast called Herr Peintinger, who crossed his Hanoverian hound known as 'Hela I' with an Istrian rough-haired hound, an event commemorated in the other native description for the breed, Peintinger bracke.

It took three generations for the type to be fixed, in a bid to create a tough, hardy breed which has since proved to be more than a match for wild boar. The rough, weather resistant coat is typically reddish, yellow of fawn in colour, as well as being short and straight. There is a tuft of longer hair on the tip of its tail.

Styrian rough-haired mountain hounds are essentially working dogs, with their breed club demanding evidence of the abilities of individuals in this respect before allowing mating to take place. Soundness is also an essential attribute, maintaining the vigour of these hounds.

The different breeds of Swiss hound are all thought to share a common ancestry, which is tied to the ancient hounds of southern Europe.

ABOVE: A Styrian rough-haired mountain hound (left), in the company of an Austrian brandlbracke.

BELOW: These hounds originate from the region of Styria in southern Austria, close to the border with the former Yugoslavia.

These are believed to have been introduced to Switzerland by the Romans. Even today, centuries later, there are distinctive similarities in appearance between the Swiss laufhunds (or scenthounds) and the Italian segugio (see page 21). The colder climate of Switzerland has meant that the laufhunds have evolved thicker coats however, becoming well adapted to their environment. Their basic appearance was already developed by the 12th century, as shown by portraits present in Zürich cathedral.

Three separate breeds of laufhund are recognised, occurring in different parts of the country. The region surrounding Berne is the home of the Berner laufhund, which can be instantly identified by its tricoloured appearance. The white areas of the coat are quite clear and show few signs of ticking. These hounds are traditionally worked in the Bernese alps, lying to the south of the city. There is also a smaller variant, identical in all respects apart from its height, called the Berner neiderlaufhund. It can be up to 10in (25cm) shorter in stature.

The Schweizer laufhund is a combination of white and shades of red, identical in height to its Berner cousin and measuring up to 23in (58cm) high at the shoulder. It played a vital part in the recreation of the porcelaine hound after the

French Revolution, emphasising the close links between the hounds in this Franco-Swiss region. A shorter-legged or neiderlaufhund form again exists, with a reputation as in other cases for having an even stronger voice than the larger variety.

All these Swiss hounds are still kept essentially for hunting purposes because of their highly active natures, although they are very friendly towards people. Their tendency to bark loudly is another drawback in more urbanised areas however, coupled with their need for plenty of exercise.

The Luzerner laufhund originates from the vicinity of Lucerne in the central northern region of the country and is characterised by its heavy ticking, which is suggestive of a close relationship with the petit bleu de Gascogne, especially as it has similar tan facial markings. The long ears, as in the case of similar breeds, hang down the sides of the neck, being relatively low set. Its smaller relative, the Luzerner neiderlaufhund, is also a popular hunting companion, being considered more agile in mountain valleys. Laufhunds in their various forms are all versatile hunters, being able to follow both fresh and cold trails.

The two Jura laufhunds originate from the vicinity of western Switzerland. The bruno Jura laufhund and the St Hubert Jura laufhund both have no white areas on their coats, being a combination of reddish-brown and black, with the black often forming a distinct saddle. The head of these hounds is very broad, with the skin being wrinkled. Combined with their coloration, this is highly suggestive of an ancestry involving the St Hubert hound. They are highly talented trackers, being used to hunt a variety of small game.

Although fewer hounds have originated in the Balkan region, they have long been prized in this part of Europe. In fact, records exist revealing how smooth-coated hounds from the Istrian peninsula, which now forms part of Slovenia, were sent to French monasteries, as they were so highly prized for their scenting skills. The Istrski gonič occurs in two distinct varieties. The kratkodlaki is the short-coated form, being a distinctive colour combination of white and orangish-tan, often with markings at the base of the tail. It is thought to be descended from a combination of European scenthound stock and sighthounds which may have been brought to the region by the Phoenicians at an early stage in history. Those individuals with thin tails are most highly valued.

The resasti or wire-coated form is similarly coloured, with a wiry coat which averages about 3in (7.5cm) or so in length over most of its body. These Istrian hounds are similarly used for hunting foxes and rabbits, as well as proving useful in detecting the presence of game. They are often kept both as companions and working hounds with a deep voice.

A number of other distinctive breeds of hound evolved within the former Yugoslavia, but their status has not been accurately determined since the region erupted into war. The Posavski gonič evolved in the north of the country, in the Posavine area around the Sava river. Individuals are wheaten through to red in colour, with white areas generally confined to the underparts and paws. The coat itself is thick and dense in texture, with the tail being quite short. These hounds, like others from this region, typically average between 18–22in (46–56cm) in height. They reputedly make good companions as well as being talented, fast hunters.

The Bosnian rough-haired hound, known as Bosanski ostrodlaki goniči-barak originated in what is now northern Bosnia over a century ago. They are well protected against the cold winters here, with a dense undercoat and a top coat which is as much as 4in (10cm) long. These hounds have been bred in a wide range of colours, ranging from single colours such as shades of yellow through to black, as well as the typical bi- and tricolours associated with hounds.

The Balksenski gonič has a short, thick and dense weather resistant coat, which is black and tan in colour. The black area may form a saddle or extend over a wider area of the back. The Balkan hound has keen tracking skills, and displays excellent stamina, revealing its location using its rather high pitched bark. It is one of the oldest breeds from the region, thought to have originated over 250 years ago and is more widely kept than others even today, although it may not be as commonly used for hunting. These pack hounds were used to pursue deer and wild boar and similar game on occasions. Its homeland is close to the eastern border of Yugoslavia and Bulgaria.

The remaining two breeds of hound face a particularly uncertain future, as they have never been especially numerous, or well represented outside the region. The Yugoslavian mountain hound, known locally as Jugoslavenski Planinski gonič originates from the Planina Mountains in the south, with the Yugoslavian tricoloured hound traditionally being found closer to the Macedonian border with Greece. They are very similar in appearance and presumably closely related although differing significantly in coloration.

The Jugoslavenski tribarini gonič is tricoloured as suggested by its English name, but ideally the white areas in the coat are restricted to the face and chest, as well as the feet and the tip of the tail. The Planinski gonič in contrast is a combination of black and tan. Both are versatile hunters, forming a strong bond with their owners. Sadly at present, they probably rank among the most endangered hound breeds in the world, but hopefully, with peace restored to the region, it may be possible to take steps to ensure their future.

Neighbouring Hungary is home to both native scenthound and sighthound breeds, which themselves survived not just war in recent times, but also active persecution as hated representations of the incursion of Hungary into Romanian territory.

The Transylvanian or Hungarian hound, called Erdelyi kopo, has an ancestry extending back to the 9th century when the Magyars crossed the Carpathian mountains on Hungary's eastern side. They brought hounds with them, which bred with those in the area, laying the foundations for this breed. The continental climate in this region – hot summers and cold winters, accompanied by heavy falls of snow – placed particular demands on hounds in terms of stamina. The breed became popular with the Hungarian aristocracy, hunting wolves and bears which used to be common in the region.

There are now two different varieties, distinguished not just by their size, but also their coloration, although neither is common. The tall Transylvanian hound stands over 22in (56cm) in height and has been favoured for hunting deer and wild boar, as well as lynx. It is black and tan in colour, whereas the short Transylvanian hound can be easily identified by its red and tan colour. Both are short-coated, with relatively coarse hair. The smaller variety hunts fox and hare, with equal vigour. These hounds have a very reliable sense of smell, plus great stamina and they also have a reputation for being quite easy to train.

The Magyar agăr or Hungarian greyhound bears a strong resemblance to the greyhound itself, being bred in an equally wide range of colours. The breed may well represent a separate ancestral line which originated somewhere in the vicinity of the eastern Mediterranean and was obtained about 1,000 years or so ago by the Magyars, who then took it to Hungary where they settled. Hungarian greyhounds have been used both legitimately for coursing and also for poaching down the course of the intervening centuries.

The breed is less refined than the greyhound, although unfortunately, widespread crossings occurred earlier this century, making the differences between the breeds less apparent. Like the Transylvanian hound, its numbers fell significantly during the Second World War, and survivors which were found were destroyed soon afterwards, as a means of purging the past in the disputed territory with Romania.

Interest in the breed grew again later, as a result of the recognition bestowed by the Fédération Cynologique International in 1966, with adherents of the breed seeking to maintain its characteristic features. In height, the Magyar agăr is slightly smaller than the greyhound itself, with a broad head and muzzle. Its coat is also less fine in texture, although the breed can still feel the cold, owing to the lack of insulation in its coat and the relative absence of fat from its body.

Fast in the field, the Magyar agăr can nevertheless make a good household companion, provided it is not allowed to pursue smaller dogs and cats. Muzzling for this purpose may be recommended.

The Greek hare hound or Hellenic hound would seem to share a common ancestry with some of the Yugoslav breeds, notably the Balkan hound itself. Known in its homeland as *Hellinikos ichnitatis*, it is predominantly black and tan in colour, sometimes with a small area of white on the chest. The breed is highly valued for its scenting abilities, with these versatile hounds being able to hunt alone or as part of a pack, often pursuing their quarry over relatively inaccessible rocky ground. They are not normally seen outside their homeland.

Another sighthound, in the guise of the Greek greyhound, can be encountered occasionally in this country, although there are very few surviving examples of the breed today. Its origins are unclear, especially as it is also described as the Albanian greyhound, but it looks rather like a saluki, with longer hair evident on the ears and tail. Rabbits and hares are the typical quarry of this coursing breed.

The Slovensky kopov is probably descended from crosses between Transylvanian hounds and other breeds, possibly even gundogs from this region. Also called the Slovakian or Black Forest hound, it took a long time for this breed to gain official recognition. This was finally granted with a standard being set in 1963. In contrast to other hounds, these dogs have a strong protective streak, making them alert guardians. The Slovensky kopov is black and tan in colour, and has a close lying hard coat which gives protection against the elements. The breed possesses great stamina and these hounds have proved to be fearless hunters of wild boar, still being used extensively for this purpose in their homeland today. They remain virtually unknown elsewhere.

The Polish hound has also not attained any strong following outside its homeland, although it is an attractive and friendly natured breed. Little is known about its origins, although it has been known under its native name of ogar Polski for roughly 300 years. Its coloration and method of working in the field are suggestive of a St Hubert hound ancestry in part, with crossings involving German hounds also contributing to the breed's development. The black-and-tan coat is short and smooth in texture, with the black area often forming a distinct saddle.

The tracking skills of the Polish hound are used primarily to locate larger game such as wild boar, while its attractive voice enables its owner to follow the hound's progress even in wooded areas. Although slightly ponderous when running, Polish hounds can move at a respectable pace. Their numbers declined dramatically as a result of the Second World War, but they have undergone a revival in recent years, and the readiness with which the breed settles in the domestic environment means that its popularity is likely to increase in the future. Unfortunately however, the smaller version of this breed, known as gonczy Polski disappeared during the 1940s.

There are four native breeds of Scandinavian hound to be found in Sweden – more than in any other country in this region. The Smalandsstövare is reputed to be the oldest, with an ancestry which dates back to the Middle Ages. It is named after the southern region of Smaland, where it hunts hares and foxes in this often thickly forested area of the country.

In spite of its long history, the Smalands hound was not officially recognised by its national kennel club until 1921, with the breed standard then being revised in 1952. These hounds are black and tan in colour, with a relatively heavy yet glossy coat. They are powerfully built, with a cobby body and strong legs. One of the most distinctive features of the Smalandsstövare is its tail however, which is unusually short. This characteristic was introduced to the breed during the 1800s by Baron von Essen, by the use of other hounds which showed this feature, and is not created by docking.

This feature is unique to the Smalandsstövare, although on occasions, puppies with longer tails still crop up in litters. The head of this breed is also relatively short, but this does not appear to compromise its scenting skills in any way. The active nature of the Smalandsstövare means that it must have plenty of exercise, so it is not suitable for an urban lifestyle.

The Schillerstövare is another old Swedish breed which dates back to the Middle Ages and could have contributed to the development of the Smalandsstövare itself. In more recent years, the pace of the Schillerstövare was improved, thanks to crosses with German hounds in particular. The breed's name commemorates that of Per Schiller, a Swedish farmer who pioneered its modern development in this way during the late 1800s.

The Schillerstövare is now probably the fastest of all Scandinavian hounds.

Schiller exhibited two examples of the breed called Tamburini and Ralla I in 1886 at the first dog show organised in the country and these hounds subsequently provided the basis for modern bloodlines, although the breed was not officially recognised until 1952. Its coloration is tan, with a black area forming the saddle.

The Schillerstövare is well suited to hunting even when there is thick snow on the ground, although its good looks mean that it is now being seen increasingly in the show ring. At present however, these hounds are rarely seen in international competitions.

One Swedish hound which is already establishing a strong following overseas, particularly in Britain, is the Hamiltonstövare. Its name commemorates that of its founder, Count Adolf Patrick Hamilton, who was also instrumental in founding the Swedish Kennel Club. He used a number of different breeds in the development of the Hamiltonstövare, some of which, such as the Curland beagle are now extinct. Foxhounds, Holsteiner, Hanover and other Germanic hounds also played a part. His efforts have resulted in one of the most popular of all Swedish breeds, thanks in part to the breed's genial nature, which makes it ideal as a companion. Its working instincts remain strong however, with plenty of opportunity for exercise being essential.

Tricoloured in appearance, with no colour predominating, the Hamiltonstövare possesses a weather resistant coat which grows considerably thicker in the winter than the summer, offering good protection against the elements. Already this breed has assumed a mythical status in its homeland thanks to a friendly house elf called Tanten, whose companion is a Hamiltonstövare known as Karo. Training of these hounds does not normally present any particular problems and their popularity seems set to grow ever more in the foreseeable future, particularly outside Sweden.

The drever is the smallest of the Swedish hounds, traditionally measuring no more than 15in (38cm) in height. It is also sometimes known as the Swedish dachsbracke, reflecting its development from the Westphalian dachsbracke (see page 107), which was introduced to both Sweden and Denmark during the early years of the 20th century. In Denmark, crossings were made with Swiss hounds, resulting in the creation of Danish dachsbracke or Strellufstöver. When these Danish hounds were brought to Sweden and crossed back to their Westphalian ancestor, the drever was born.

Its name originates from the Swedish *drev*, meaning 'to hunt', and it has proved to be a very versatile tracking dog, as well as a lively companion. Although the drever's short legs mean that the breed is not especially fast when working, it displays tremendous stamina and dedication to its task.

The drever was first recognised by the Swedish Kennel Club in 1949 and achieved equivalent recognition seven years later in Canada, although the breed is not especially well represented elsewhere in the world at present. Its coloration can be variable, with both fawn and white and tricolours being commonly seen. White areas should be confined to the face, neck, chest, legs and tip of the tail.

The Hygenhund is one of Norway's oldest hounds, evolved during the late 1800s by an enthusiast called Hygen. He used Holsteiner hounds from Germany as the main basis for the breed, along with others of Scandinavian origin including the now extinct Ringerike hound. The aim was to create hounds with excellent stamina and there are some obvious similarities with the Swedish Smalandsstövare apparent in the Hygenhund today. These include its relatively short body and tail, as well as its rather short, broad head. It exists in a variety of colours, based on combinations of shades of red, black and white. Still kept and highly valued for its hunting abilities, the Hygenhund is used primarily to track hares. It has never become popular simply as a companion, probably because of its temperament and so is not especially common, even in its homeland.

The Dunker is another Norwegian breed named after its creator, which came into being during the first half of the 19th century. It resulted from crosses between the Russian harlequin hound and other hounds in the region, thanks to the

Norwegian elkhound. Unrelated to the main hound lineage, this Nordic breed is actually a member of the spitz family of breeds.

endeavours of Wilhelm Dunker. The input from the Russian bloodline is clearly apparent today in the very distinctive appearance of this breed. A number of individuals display the dappled blue merle appearance with some solid patches of black, plus tan and white areas on the coat. Such hounds can show the blue or 'glass' eye arising from the presence of this gene, which is generally rare amongst hound breeds, with a few exceptions such as the mountain cur from the USA and dachshunds.

It is important to pair such individuals to those which do not have the blue merle gene in their make-up, simply because otherwise the resulting puppies can suffer from a high incidence of deafness, often being predominantly white in colour. The coat itself is dense, affording good protection against the cold. There was a time when the lighter Dunker was crossed with the Hygenhund, with a view to developing a third type of hound, called the Norwegian beagle. This attempt did not achieve great support however, and ultimately failed. Although also known as the Norwegian hound, the Dunker has only a small following outside its homeland, which is perhaps strange, given the striking patterning and pleasant nature of these hounds.

The Haldenstövare is the most recent breed of hound to have been evolved successfully in Norway, with its origins dating back to the 1950s. Its name is derived from the southern town of Halden where a variety of breeds such as English foxhounds and others from various European countries were used in its development. The Haldenstövare has a distinctive tricoloured coat, in which white coloration usually predominates. Tall and relatively light, it is highly athletic, although perhaps not so hardy as some other breeds from this part of the world. As with other Scandinavian hounds, this breed tends to hunt with its owner on an individual basis. It also makes a good companion, being affectionate by nature, but it remains quite rare, even in Norway.

Also of recent origin is the Strellufstöver or Danish dachsbracke. This breed was created by Frands Frandsen, who lived at Holsted on Jutland. He sought to develop hounds which would prove effective hunters in his home area, and used the Westphalian dachsbracke, Smalandsstövare and Berner laufhunds in his quest, which began in 1912. Just over a decade later he had achieved his ambition, with the Strellufstöver having established an enviable reputation with hunters throughout Denmark and further afield.

A breed club was established in 1929 and the prefix of Strelluf was chosen as the basis of the breed's name, being derived from that of Frandsen's kennel. In due course the Strellufstöver contributed to the breeding of the drever, which it closely resembles, although its following today is significantly smaller than that of its Swedish relative.

The Finnish hound, referred to as Suomenajokoira in its homeland, represents a mixture of English, German and Swiss breeds, along with those from Scandinavia. It was developed in the 18th century by a goldsmith called Tammelin. Showing a typical tricoloured patterning, it has acquired a reputation as an independent and affable companion, which will track not only live quarry but also locate the whereabouts of shot game birds such as woodcock. Finnish hounds have yet to make an impression on the show scene, being kept primarily as working companions.

The Baltic states are home to three distinctive

Finnish spitz, a breed characterised by its striking orangish-red colour. It has the prick-ears and curled tail, and is not a true hound.

breeds of hound. The gontchaja Estonskaja originates from Estonia, where it was developed during the first half of the 20th century. Prior to this, large hounds had been used to hunt the native goats of the region, with the aim then being to create a small breed which would not be able to take the goats, but could outrun foxes and hares.

The smaller hounds were crossed with beagles for this purpose and then Swiss neiderlaufhund stock was added, to improve the persistence and voice of the emerging breed and increase its maturity. The resulting breed was awarded a standard in 1954. It is typically black and tan in colour, with powerful legs and an alert demeanour, which often means that it is used as a guardian and household companion. Examples of the Estonian hound are virtually unknown even today however, outside its homeland.

The same applies in the case of the other two Baltic breeds. The Latvian hound was developed to locate game in the often densely forested landscape of Latvia, participating in a particularly unique style of hunting. A specified area of forest was blocked off, with hunters only permitted to shoot their quarry when it crossed open paths. They relied on what were called Curland hounds up until 1920 to assist them, with these canine companions having to be particularly responsive as to what was required of them. They were derived from English, Swiss and Polish hound stock.

A ban on using hounds taller than 20in (51cm) in height resulted in hunters then seeking Curland and dachshund crosses, which were often mated with beagles. Finally an official breeding programme was set up and in 1977 a standard was drawn up for these hounds. The Latvian hound is black and tan in colour, measures 19in (48cm) or less at the shoulder and has a rather basset-like appearance, although its legs are straight. Obedience is a particular feature of these hounds, given their style of hunting.

The Lithuanian hound represents a modern attempt to recreate the old Curland hound, using local breeds of hound and others from further afield, including the St Hubert and Polish hounds. The number of these scent hounds fell perilously low during the 1970s, before the Lithuanian Cynological Council undertook to assist the breeding programme. The resulting hounds of today are predominantly black in colour, with some tan markings and stand up to 24in (61cm) tall.

Lithuania's near neighbour, Russia, is home to one of the most famous of all sighthounds, the borzoi or Russian wolfhound. This breed was greatly favoured by the Russian aristocracy before the revolution and has since become popular throughout the world. Across the huge expanse of the former Soviet Union, there used to be a number of recognised strains, such as the Turkman borzoi, chortaj and tasy which may still exist in certain areas today, although such distinctions have long since disappeared in the breed elsewhere in the world.

Their origins date back to the 17th century, when sighthounds from Arabia were brought to Russia for hunting purposes. The initial attempts were unsuccessful, with the imported hounds apparently succumbing to the cold of their adoptive homeland. Subsequent attempts yielded better results however, and crossings involving native coursing breeds resulted in hardier hounds which proved suitably adept at hunting wolves, with great ceremonial pageant.

Borzois were trained to hunt as couples, matched in terms of coloration to please the eye of the onlookers and in speed to ensure their safety and a successful outcome. Both hounds were required to seize the wolf simultaneously, overpowering it and holding it on the ground so that it could be killed by a strike of a nobleman's dagger at close quarters, or sometimes even muzzled.

After attracting much attention in England during the 1880s, the first examples of this breed were then taken to the USA in 1889, where its aristocratic elegance meant that it was soon highly prized. A keen supporter of the breed, Joseph B. Thomas then journeyed to Russia from the USA in 1903 in search of traditional examples of the breed. His quest was rewarded at the kennels of both the Grand Duke Nicholas, located at Tula, and Artem Balderoff in Woronzova. The borzois obtained from these sources were to have a major impact on the subsequent development of the breed on both sides of the Atlantic.

Borzois hunted in matched pairs, running either side of a wolf in order to overpower it with relative safety.

The turmoil arising as a result of the Russian Revolution in 1917 then resulted in the breeding of these hounds in their homeland almost ceasing entirely for a period. Their links with the despised Romanoffs meant that they suffered direct persecution as well as neglect.

In the west, the borzoi, although not kept for hunting purposes, has prospered in the show ring since those days and is also now valued as a companion. These hounds tend to have a rather imperious nature however, and are not an ideal choice for a home alongside boisterous children. Their silky, flat and wavy or curly coat must have regular grooming, to prevent any tangles developing in it. The coat coloration is not specified for show purposes, with borzois being bred in a wide range of colours. Prominent white areas are often apparent. As might be anticipated, borzois need the opportunity to run freely off the leash every day, being exercised away from roads and livestock, just in case their hunting instincts return.

Borzois today are kept essentially as companions, rather than for hunting purposes. They are very popular in the show ring, although they must be well-trained to stop them misbehaving in these surroundings.

The borzoi's elegant profile results in part from the long, slender shape of its head, with its ears being quite small. The deep chest reveals the breed's hunting ancestry, providing for a good lung capacity. Longer hair extends down the backs of the front and hind legs. This so-called feathering partly disguises the powerful limbs, which terminate in hare-shaped feet, affording a good grip even when turning at speed thanks to their surface area.

Borzois are still being kept in Russia, and the breed appears to be undergoing something of a resurgence of popularity there at present, with the Russian Cyndronic Association maintaining a list of such hounds. Emphasis is being placed on recreating the regional variants of the borzoi as far as possible. The term 'borzoi' is actually a generic term in Russian for sighthounds, rather than describing an individual type.

The tasy, also called the mid-Asiatic borzoi, reflecting its centre of origin in the states of Uzbekistan, Kazakhstan and Turkmenistan, has been kept in this region for centuries. It may be linked not just with the borzoi, but also the Afghan hound (see page 121) whose homeland is in neighbouring Afghanistan. The tasy is an elegant if unrefined breed, compared with its two internationally recognised relatives. Its coat is noticeably shorter, although there are traces of feathering on the back of the front legs and the ears. In terms of coloration these hounds are often tan, frequently broken with areas of black. Grey individuals are also seen quite frequently and white markings are not uncommon.

Although primarily a sighthound, the tasy also possesses quite a keen sense of smell, enabling it to work in a wider range of habitats than traditionally associated with sighthounds, within the confines of areas of forest for example. Tradition dictates that the tasy is also sometimes hunted in combination with eagles over suitable terrain, with the bird harrying the quarry, assisting the hound to catch it.

The taigan, sometimes spelt tajgan, occurs further east, close to the Chinese border. Here it is to be found in the mountainous region of the Tian Shan mountains of Kirghizia, and so is also sometimes called the Kirghizia borzoi. The breed used to exist in a wide range of colours, ranging from white and shades of fawn through greys to black. White markings are also to be seen on some individuals. Unfortunately, it appears that the numbers of these hounds has fallen significantly over recent years, although as with the tasy, the Russian Kennel Club is working hard to ensure their survival. The taigan is also pitched against a wide range of game, ranging from marmots to wolves, and shows a similar if not superior versatility in its hunting habits, even having a reputation for retrieving game.

The steppe borzoi has evolved in the vast open landscape to the west of the Caspian sea, where pace is a priority for any hunting breed. These borzois are especially fast, being capable of bursts of rapid acceleration, with older hounds being used to train their younger companions in the art of turning quarry. The South Russian steppe hound, as this breed is also known, occurs in solid colours. Like the other Russian sighthounds, its ultimate ancestry probably extends back as far as ancient Persia and thence to the original lineage of the Middle East.

On occasions, these borzois are hunted in conjunction with the chortaj, which has arisen in the same area and may actually have contributed to the development of the steppe borzoi. It is sometimes called the eastern greyhound, although in appearance it is in effect a smooth-coated borzoi, bred in a wide range of colours. There is no stop down its face, marking a delineation between forehead and nose, with the ears of the chortaj being small.

The vision of these hounds is particularly acute. They are said to be able to detect their quarry at a distance as far away as 280yd (256m). The chortaj, whose name is pronounced 'hortai' is now starting to be seen occasionally on the show scene in Russia, suggesting that it may become more widely known again in the future.

Russia is also home to two breeds of scenthound, one of which is described under the unusual name of the Russian drab yellow hound, because of its distinctive coloration. It is yellowish-red in colour, sometimes with a black saddle and occasional small white patches of hair, being known as gontchaja Russkaja in its homeland. Its origins probably date back as far as the Middle Ages, with the breed being developed from European hound stock crossed with the Russian herding dogs called laikas.

In the past, the Russian drab yellow hound was kept in packs for hunting purposes, with the calls of these hounds being sufficiently individual for huntsmen to recognise them from afar on this basis. Today however, they tend to be used for hunting on their own, with hares and, to a lesser extent, foxes being their principal quarry. The breed possesses good scenting abilities and stamina, which combined with its friendly nature, has made it very popular in its homeland.

There used to be various different strains of this hound, and these were often distinguished by different regional names. The official standard however, drawn up in 1925 reflected the appearance of those hounds originating from the Kostroma region, which is why the breed is also sometimes called the Kostroma hound in the west.

During the 19th century, the Russian drab yellow hound was crossed with foxhound stock brought from England to create what became known initially as the Anglo-Russian hound. This name was then changed in 1951 to that of the Russian harlequin hound or gontchaja Russkaja pegaja, reflecting its tricoloured appearance. They were initially used to track game so that once it had broken cover, the quicker borzoi hounds could be released to run the quarry down, but in due course they were kept exclusively for hunting on their own.

Russian harlequin hounds were then pitched against wolves and foxes, proving adept at hunting them. One of the most widely acclaimed packs of recent years is that kept by the Dynamo Sport Society of Tula, which has had a significant impact on modern bloodlines of the breed. The Russian harlequin hound is now being seen with increasing frequency in the show ring in its homeland. Its short, dense coat helps to emphasise the clarity of its markings. In terms of type, it is more compact than the Russian hound and may be slightly smaller in height.

Several other breeds of sighthound are to be found in parts of southern Asia. By far the best known of these is the Afghan hound, which has established an immense international following. This breed is known locally in its homeland as tazi and bears a strong resemblance to the Russian tasy, although the ancestors of both probably originated in North Africa. Their geographical proximity means they could well have evolved from the same ancestral stock. In fact, a number of regional forms of the Afghan existed, as was apparent when the early examples of the breed were introduced to Europe and North America. Those which originated from mountainous areas had thicker, more profuse coats than those from more lowland parts of the country.

The Afghan hound only has short hair on its face, whereas over the rest of the body, the coat is long.

ABOVE: The coloration of the Afghan hound shows many variations, although the nose is usually black.

BELOW: The topknot of long hair is a particular feature of the Afghan, extending back down over the ears.

The first member of the breed to be imported to Britain, called Zardin, was obtained by an army officer, Captain Banff, and caused something of a sensation when exhibited at the Crystal Palace show in 1907. Agile and graceful, the Afghan is well suited to its rugged environment, being able to run at speed thanks to its high standing, broad hips and large feet, which together act like shock absorbers. The tail is a particularly distinctive feature of the breed, being low-set and curled at its tip.

The pace of the Afghan allows it to run down gazelles – the fastest members of the antelope tribe in its homeland – while the breed's natural bravery means that it will tackle wolves as well as foxes. It is kept partly as a guardian of flocks of sheep and goats in Afghanistan but is valued both as a companion and show dog in the west. As bloodlines have been developed here, so the coats of these hounds have become more profuse, making regular daily grooming imperative. These are very demanding hounds to keep in good condition, as their coats will mat readily.

Like other sighthounds, they are also not especially responsive to training and should be watched when being exercised in the vicinity of smaller dogs, in case their hunting instincts take

In the case of young Afghans, the coat is shorter at first, especially in the topknot and saddle areas.

The Afghan hound retains its athletic ability, possessing strong forelegs and powerful hindquarters.

over. Muzzling may be advisable under such circumstances. Afghans are very affectionate and exuberant hounds however, particularly when in the company of those whom they know well, and are quite at home in domestic surroundings, provided that they are given plenty of opportunity for exercise.

It has been suggested that the ancient Rampur greyhound from India might also be related to the Afghan hound, as it is known that these hounds were taken into what is present-day India long before they became known in the west. Even so, the appearance of the Rampur greyhound today is more reflective of the relatively recent greyhound crosses undertaken in the 19th century to improve the pace of this breed. It is named after the Indian state of Rampur where its development occurred. The size of these hounds is quite variable, and they appear rare today, even in their homeland, although the breed has been introduced to Canada.

The other breeds of Indian greyhound, called Banjara and Mahratta are also scarce and not standardised. The Banjara has arisen in the north-west of the country, being associated with the Banjara people who live in the state of Rajasthan. It is a rough coated breed, typically bred in solid colours such as wheaten, or in a brindle form, with its precise ancestry being unclear.

Another Asiatic breed based in part on greyhound stock is the kangaroo hound of Australia. It is the only hound breed native to this continent, created in the mid-1880s. The settlers' aim was to create a breed which would have the pace to outrun and catch these marsupials and sufficiently strong to be able to hold them without being injured by their sharp claws. Deerhound and Irish wolfhound stock were used for this purpose, creating what could also be described as a longdog. These kangaroo hounds were bred in a variety of colours, reflecting their ancestry. Brindles, blacks and bicolours were common.

Over recent years however, the numbers of such hounds appears to have fallen greatly, to the stage where they may already have died out. Being kept essentially for hunting purposes only, there was never any attempt made to standardise the breed and so it did not develop or command interest in show circles, which could have ensured its survival.

For many years the only breed of ridgeback well known to hound enthusiasts around the world was the Rhodesian ridgeback (see page 30). Yet for over a thousand years, the Thai ridgeback has been kept in south-east Asia, certainly in both Thailand and Cambodia, based on cave paintings portraying hounds of this type. It is also known as the Phu Quoc dog, taking its name from an island in the Gulf of Siam, which is now Vietnamese territory. This is where the first of these dogs was seen by westerners in the 19th century.

Thai ridgebacks have proven to be very versatile in their homeland, being kept for hunting a variety of game, working more as sighthounds than scenthounds. They are also valued for guarding property.

It appears that there are a number of distinctive lineages of such hounds, based on the appearance of the ridge of hair. Recent genetic studies have helped to highlight Thailand as the centre of its origins, since the examples of the breed encountered here have the widest and longest ridges, extending across the vertebral column and even to the flanks in some cases, compared with those from elsewhere, such as Vietnam. The ancestral stock is then likely to have been taken from the ports on the eastern seaboard to other parts of the region, such as Indonesia.

What cannot be resolved as yet however, is whether the Thai ridgeback was introduced early in history to east Africa, laying the foundations for the Hottentot dog and ultimately the Rhodesian ridgeback. It is certain though that the Thai ridgeback is the direct and largely unaltered descendant of a primitive dingo-type hunting dog of south-eastern Asia.

A highly athletic breed, the Thai ridgeback has a reputation for being able to jump exceptionally well. These hounds have large triangular-shaped ears which tilt forward slightly, and wrinkled skin on the forehead, creating the impression of intense concentration. The breed exists in a variety of solid colour forms, including fawn, chestnut-red, blue (which is a silver form) and black, with the coat itself being smooth.

The Thai ridgeback first achieved recognition in its homeland, with the Fédération Cynologique International then granting it international status in 1993. It is now becoming increasingly well known in the USA, where it was first imported to California by a breeder called Jack Sterling, as well as in Japan. The number of these ridgebacks being kept abroad remains small at present however, compared with the number in Thailand itself. Here it is relatively common, to the extent that it is known as Meh Thai which means simply 'Thai dog'.

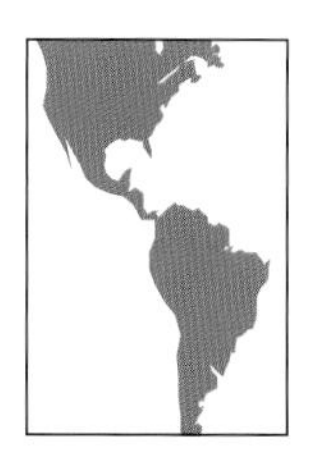

CHAPTER 7

THE HOUNDS OF THE AMERICAS

The grey wolf still maintains a wide distribution across North America, particularly in the far north of the continent. While those dogs native to this part of the continent, such as the Alaskan malamute, still bear a strong resemblance to wolves, being well-adapted to surviving in what is an inhospitable climate, they were not generally kept primarily for hunting purposes.

There were exceptions however, such as the Tahltan bear dog, raised by the Tahltan Indian tribe in Canada. These were brave but small hounds, measuring a maximum of 15in (38cm) at the shoulder, and weighing no more than 15lb (6.7kg). Their homeland was in the vicinity of the north-western part of British Columbia, extending into the southern part of the Yukon Territory. The origins of these dogs is essentially unknown, although contemporary European accounts of the 17th century describe how they lived closely with their owners, sharing their tents.

Tahltan bear dogs did not bark, but rather like the basenji of Africa, they uttered yodelling calls. They would also yap loudly when confronting a bear. Their coats were short and dense, to give them protection against the bitter cold, but their tails were their most unusual feature. These were short and bushy, with the hair at the tip being sprayed out rather like a shaving brush.

Prior to a hunt, these dogs were ritually stabbed in their hindquarters with a dagger-like fibula bone from a bear or wolf until they bled. Tahltan bear dogs were used in couples, carried over the snow in sacks until a bear's trail was spotted. They were then released to chase after the bear, bounding over the snow until they caught up with the unfortunate animal. They would seek to harry the bear as it sank further into the snow, allowing the hunters to get close enough to kill it. On occasions, Tahltan bear dogs were also used to pursue big cats such as lynx in a similar way, being scratched with a claw on their face as a ritual beforehand in this instance.

It appears that these small hounds were doomed to extinction by their unique lifestyle. The introduction of other dogs to the region spelt disaster, as Tahltan bear dogs proved to be highly susceptible to distemper, while attempts to transpose them elsewhere were unsuccessful. They did not adapt well to life in milder climates, and they were very finicky regarding food, eating only small quantities and often succumbing to digestive disorders. Although the Canadian Kennel Club extended recognition to the breed in 1941, it appears that it is now extinct. By 1984, there were only two spayed Tahltan bear dogs still known to be alive.

Ritual was a very important aspect of hunting for the tribespeople of the Americas, and since their survival could depend on a successful outcome, it would often appear to be extreme and cruel. While the Tahltans stabbed their dogs until blood was drawn, the Thompsons would steam and bathe their hounds as they would themselves, before setting out on the hunt. Rituals practised by other tribes included the provision of special drinks and even the administration of hallucinogenic drugs to dogs prior to a hunt. The Waiwai tribespeople believed that by placing pepper juice in the eyes of their hounds, they would then hunt better, being forced to rely on their sense of smell, as the result of having been temporarily blinded in this fashion.

The earliest clear evidence of dogs being used for hunting in this part of the world is derived from rock art dating back as early as 200 BC, found in the Coso Range within the states of Nevada and California. These petroglyphs reveal that dogs were being used to hunt the bighorn sheep roaming in the Great Basin of the USA at that stage. These hounds are more reminiscent of a sighthound rather than a scenthound, having raised ears and a long tail, plus relatively short legs.

Although this probably meant that they could not outrun their quarry, the hunting techniques employed by the tribespeople of the region relied upon simply driving the sheep either into nets, or towards waiting hunters, hidden from view. In some areas the quarry was driven off cliffs, enabling injured individuals or those killed by the fall to be taken below. The hounds were sometimes kept on rope leashes, so that in their enthusiastic pursuit of the sheep, they could not follow them over a precipice.

While hunting in North America appears to have been undertaken to provide food for the Indian communities, there is some evidence from further south that it could have developed into a sport at an early stage in history. The Mayas used hounds to hunt deer, according to contemporary portrayals driving them into nets, with members of the ruling aristocracy featuring in such scenes. Similar hunts were organised by the Moche tribe, which inhabited the coastal region of Peru at the same time, from roughly 200–800 AD.

Early European accounts refer to dogs which were kept for a variety of purposes, often having to scavenge for themselves and proving quite aggressive by nature. In the far north, as elsewhere, dogs were kept for a variety of reasons, rather than just for hunting. The Iglulik for example, relied on their dogs to help them locate and hunt musk oxen. After a successful kill, the dogs were then used to haul the meat back to the settlement. The keeping of dogs therefore enhanced the prospects of survival, in what would become a bitterly cold and hostile environment during the long winter period.

There is evidence of dogs being taken south, even before European settlement began. There were hounds in what is now California during this period, which were about the size of a small foxhound, black and white in colour with raised ears.

The hounds in this area were typically used to catch small quarry such as rabbits and even squirrels. On occasions, they would be used to drive elk and deer to places where these creatures could be trapped and ambushed. There was often a wide range of attitudes to dogs among such tribes. The Shasta Indians built special huts for their hounds close to their own and would sing to them, using special songs which were believed to improve the scenting power of the dogs. In contrast however, the southern Yokut kept dogs essentially as a source of food, rather than for their ability to provide a more varied menu.

On the plains of North America, life changed significantly with the advent of European exploration, and particularly the introduction of the horse. Up until this stage, the tribespeople there had been forced to hunt on foot with their dogs, but now it was possible to pursue the buffalo (bison) much more effectively on horseback. The dogs themselves were probably fed in part on pemmican, which is a mixture of buffalo meat beaten into thin strips and allowed to dry in the sun, to which various dried berries and other ingredients may be added.

In some societies however, hounds were not permitted to benefit from their kills. The Montagnais tribe prevented their dogs from gnawing on the bones of caribou, ostensibly because it would make them ill, but in reality this behaviour was disallowed because of the deeply-held belief that the caribou would sense the dog's treachery, having turned against the other animals by assisting people in the hunt. Similar beliefs were quite widespread elsewhere on the continent, as in the culture of the Cree Indians. Their hounds were never fed any morsels of the resulting meal after a hunt, but rather all inedible remains were burnt.

For many years their dogs were also used to haul the remains back to the camp, and this continued until well into the 19th century, by which stage dogs of European origins had begun to breed on quite a wide scale with those resident in North America, altering their appearance away from the prick-eared dogs which often resembled coyotes (*Canis latrans*).

The first settlers in the Caribbean originated from northern South America, and brought small dogs with them. Since the wolf did not range this far south and bearing in mind the size of these canids, it is possible that they could be descended from the rather unusual bush dog (*Speothos venaticus*), which only stands about 30cm (12in) tall at the shoulder. Even today in parts of South America, young of this species are kept by Indian tribespeople and can become quite tame, to the extent of rolling over and having their underparts stroked, just like a domestic dog.

Bush dogs have a more varied range of vocalisations than the dog or indeed the grey wolf, frequently uttering high-pitched calls and whining rather than attempting to bark. This may have been a feature of these early Caribbean dogs. Both Columbus, when he arrived in the region during 1492, and subsequent chroniclers such as Acosta just over a century later, described these small dogs kept by the Taino people as aons. The aon was soon exterminated by the European invaders however, who, although noting its hunting abilities, preferred to eat these unusual dogs.

There was also another slightly larger type of hunting dog in this region. It appears to have been used to catch the large rodents called hutias, which were formerly quite widely distributed through the Caribbean region, but are decidedly uncommon today.

Although now diluted by the numerous cross-breedings which have occurred with the European dogs brought to the islands over the centuries, it is still possible in the Greater Antilles to detect signs of their former dominance, most notably in the brindled coats of the so-called *satos* dogs living there. Although generalisations are

Bush dog (Speothos venaticus). A rather unusual wild canid that is kept in some parts of South America.

difficult, because of the paucity of the evidence, it appears that the dogs found on some of these islands were larger than those which inhabited others, based on the limited skeletal material which still survives.

Before long however, the scenting skills of European hounds were being employed to keep local people in a perpetual state of fear. Tales were told, often with justification, of how such hounds were fed on human flesh to maintain their antipathy to those whom they were tracking. Philip II of Spain (1556–98) is credited with starting this means of locating runaway slaves and others.

It appears that such hounds, originally developed from the St Hubert lineage (see page 37), were soon crossed with mastiff stock, to raise their level of aggression so that they would unhesitatingly attack people, rather like the alaunt of medieval times. These so-called Cuban hounds were greatly feared, for good reason. Following a mutiny aboard a British ship off the island of Cuba, which resulted in the deaths of all the officers, the sailors involved landed on the island, heading to the dense interior where they thought they could escape justice by going over the mountains to the south of the island.

The enraged governor of the island dispatched a dozen *chasseurs* (dog-handlers) with their feared Cuban hounds in pursuit of the renegades. These men were dedicated to their task and on the government payroll, which was probably essential, given the cost of feeding the three hounds which every chasseur was obliged to have, although they were only used as couples.

It appears that Cuban bloodhounds were not especially talented as trackers, which in turn suggests they were more likely to be of mastiff rather than true bloodhound descent. In fact they were accompanied by 'finder' dogs whose role was to find the scent for them. They could then pursue their quarry. The aggressive nature of the Cuban hounds was emphasised by the fact that they were kept muzzled and were trained to attack as soon as they were allowed off the leash.

The mystique and fear surrounding the breed was greatly enhanced by the exploits of these twelve chasseurs and their hounds who rounded up all the mutineers and brought them back alive to Havana, where they were hanged. Their value was further confirmed following a revolt by the Maroons, who were free descendants of former slaves, living alongside the British on Jamaica.

General Walpole, commanding the British, sought the assistance of the Cuban *chasseurs* and their hounds, to stamp out the rebellion. The force of 40 *chasseurs* and just 104 hounds arrived at Kingston, after a journey across the Caribbean which lasted seven weeks. The hounds immediately inspired fear in the local populace and ended up nearly attacking General Walpole and the horses that were pulling his post-chaise in their exuberance, when a demonstration of their ability to work under gunfire was arranged soon afterwards. The mere presence of these hounds on the island was sufficient to result in the Maroons' surrender, without any need for them to enter the field.

Hounds had also been brought to the mainland of North America at an early stage in European settlement of the continent. It is now thought that the pack of 'English hounds' kept by Robert Brooke in Maryland, which was one of the first in the New World, was actually comprised of the ancient Kerry beagle (see page 86), a breed of Irish descent. Contemporary descriptions reveal these hounds to have been black and tan in colour, rather than tri-coloured like foxhounds. They were often pitted against the grey fox (*Urocyan cinereoargenteus*), which has shorter legs and so is less speedy than its red relative, although it is an agile climber, as reflected by its alternative name of tree-climbing fox.

It was only after the introduction of the red fox (*Vulpes vulpes*) to the USA, for the purposes of hunting, that English-type foxhounds grew in popularity. Red foxes occurred naturally in some parts of the continent, with the species having a holoarctic distribution, but the purpose of the various introductions of these foxes from Europe was to provide hunting opportunities for the settlers in areas which had not been colonised by the species at that stage.

These introductions began about 1650, when eight pairs were brought from Liverpool on an English tobacco schooner and liberated in a coastal strip of Maryland. They were soon breeding successfully, but they did not spread into neighbouring Virginia until after the bitter winter of 1679–80. Other releases were made in a fairly haphazard fashion for over a century, and today, the red fox population in the south-eastern part of the USA is derived predominantly from these imports, rather than indigenous stock.

It is no surprise therefore, that this region in turn has also served as the cradle for most of America's hound breeds. The majority have been bred from English foxhounds, which were soon used to pursue the red fox in its new surroundings. Gradually however, the appearance of the pack hounds began to change, as reflected by the American foxhound of today.

At first glance, this breed could be confused with its English relative, but the American foxhound is slightly taller, with a lighter body. This increase in stride length means that they are potentially slightly faster when pursuing their quarry. During the late 18th and early 19th centuries, both individuals such as George Washington and organisations like the Gloucester Fox-hunting Club sought to obtain stock representative of the best English bloodlines from Britain.

Much emphasis was placed on the coloration of these evolving lineages in the USA, dating back to the early 1800s. The description of 'July' was applied to foxhounds of a solid tan coloration, with this name still being in use today. These hounds in turn contributed to the development of Colonel Haiden Trigg's blue-ticked hounds, with their distinctive white collars. They were so unusual that many initially regarded them as a separate breed, rather than simply as a colour variant. Even today, there are packs distinguished by the coloration of their foxhounds, such as the black and tan, which is characteristic of the Penn Marrydales.

As in Britain, such foxhounds are still kept primarily for hunting purposes, rather than being seen in the show ring. In the field, American foxhounds have proved to be fast and talented trackers in pursuit of their quarry, often being described as 'hot nosed' which reflects their ability to follow the scent of a fox racing before them.

Nevertheless, it was not just English foxhounds that had an influence on the development of hound breeds in the USA. Such was the landscape and the life style of the early settlers that the ancestral foxhound-type stock became more diversified. Fox hunting may have been a pastime in some areas of the country, but in others, reliance on a sound hunting dog could literally make the difference between survival and death.

More in keeping with the situation in France or elsewhere in Continental Europe, there was a requirement for hounds which could be worked either singly or in small groups, on foot. In some instances, they were also required as guardians, protecting both against attacks by animals and by hostile Indians, in addition to hunting.

Such hounds played a vital role in the settlement of North America, accompanying the European immigrants as they headed west, but by the nature of their life style, their evolution into a settled, standardised breed was unlikely. Today, the leopard cur is the best-known representative of this group, but even so, it has yet to achieve official recognition at the time of writing from the American Kennel Club. Although the description of 'cur' tends to suggest a mongrel, it is an abbreviation of 'cur-tailed' in this case. The early examples of the leopard cur were naturally semi tail-less, and this, combined with its merle or spotted patterning led to the unusual name of these hounds.

The appearance of the leopard cur is not sufficiently distinctive to allow its ancestry to be worked out with any certainty however, simply because a number of different European breeds were brought to the USA, all of whom have this distinctive patterning. Records suggest that the first were introduced by the Spanish as early as 1542, to be followed by various French hounds, not to mention the Beauceron, which had been bred originally for hunting wild boar before being kept for herding purposes.

Other stock dogs, including the blue merle collie, were also introduced to the vicinity of North Carolina in the south-eastern part of the USA where the leopard cur was first bred. What is clear is that both herding dogs and hounds contributed to its development, making it a versatile and adaptable companion, at home on a farmstead or hunting. The leopard cur's origins meant that these dogs were instinctively drawn to

ABOVE: Leopard cur. This is a black-and-tan individual. Crosses with herding dogs have shaped their character.

These curs are widely kept on farmsteads in the southern states, originating from southern Carolina.

work with people, proving easier and more responsive to train compared with most hounds.

A more unusual feature, which has since been transposed into a number of other American breeds of hound, is the way in which the leopard cur displays a natural tendency to drive creatures which it is pursuing, such as squirrels and raccoons, up into trees. Such behaviour is known as treeing, although why it should have become so highly developed in the case of the leopard cur remains a mystery.

Since leopard curs were bred very much as working dogs, it was inevitable that as the environment in which they were developed gradually changed, so their place in the world appeared to be less certain. Breeders have quite consciously selected for working abilities, rather than features such as coloration. Although the merle pattern is most often associated with the leopard cur, black-and-tan individuals are not uncommon either, while odd brindles and yellows are among the other colour variants sometimes encountered.

Areas of white hair, typically in the vicinity of the neck or the points, including the tail, are not unusual. As a result of the peculiarities associated with the merle gene however, merle individuals are never paired together, because of the risk of deaf and/or blind white puppies arising in the litter. Out-crossing to these other colours is therefore essential.

Unfortunately, some unscrupulous breeders took advantage of the dominant nature of the merle gene, and crossed leopard curs with other hounds, as a means of boosting their numbers. This was possible because the resulting puppies all had the characteristic coloration, and with relatively little emphasis on type, so these hybrids ended up being described as leopard curs.

There have been noticeable changes in the breed down the centuries in any event. Most puppies today are born with full length tails, unlike their ancestors. These are not docked. Today, there are two organisations, the American Cur Breeders Association, founded in 1959, and the Leopard Tree Dog Registration Office, set up during 1977, both of which are dedicated to the survival of this unusual hound. The pedigrees of the leopard curs registered with them are of genuine ancient lineage, and can be traced back to North Carolina stock.

Their relatively broad muzzles reveal their keen scenting abilities, although they tend to indicate their position when in pursuit of quarry by barking rather than baying like most scent hounds. Having treed game, they will wait at the base of the tree, barking to ensure the creature remains there until their handler catches up with them. Leopard curs have proved to be exceedingly loyal dogs and they can display considerable stamina, being able to work in both very hot and cold spells of weather.

The multi-purpose aspects of the curs is further reflected in the case of the Catahoula cur, also known as the Catahoula leopard dog. It was adopted as Louisiana's state dog in 1979, with its unusual name being derived from the Parish of Catahoula. These curs occur in both merle and black-and-tan colour variants.

In contrast to the leopard cur however, tracking and herding skills predominate in this dog's nature. It is especially valued for rounding up wild hogs, sometimes being described as the Catahoula hog dog for this reason. This calls for both resourcefulness and bravery on the part of such dogs, because boar of this type are formidable adversaries if challenged. The dogs will track the hogs, nipping those at the rear. This then results in the other hogs turning to defend their fellows. They would seek to pursue the dogs, who would lead them into a pen nearby, where the gate could be slammed shut, trapping the hogs while the dogs escaped.

The scenting abilities of the Catahoula leopard dog are also employed in searching for cattle which have wandered off over a wide area of scrubland. They will then drive them back, snapping determinedly at their heels rather like

Catahoula leopard dog. The mottled coloration of these dogs is believed to originate from French hound stock.

ABOVE: The Catahoula leopard dog is powerfully built, and able to run at speed, as well as displaying considerable stamina.

ABOVE: In addition to hunting, the pace of these dogs is used for rounding up farmstock, reflecting the herding aspect of their ancestry.

LEFT: Its broad chest and powerful feet contribute to the athletic ability of the Catahoula leopard dog.

Welsh Corgis. Catahoula leopard dogs will also hunt raccoons, like other hounds from this area, and possess a baying call, not dissimilar to European hounds. They do not take readily to strangers, proving determined guardians of property.

Curs are far from standardised in appearance, as reflected by the size of the black mouth cur, which can vary from 16–25in (40–64cm) at the shoulder, and from 40–95lb (20–43kg) in weight! In this case however, the muzzle is typically black, as its name suggests, while the coat itself can vary from a slightly reddish shade of yellow through to fawn. There may be some white areas present over the feet in particular, as well as on the chest and at the tip of the tail.

These dogs have a very solid, muscular build and display great stamina. Their gait is unusual, passing from a walk to a loping run, rather than trotting at any stage. Although they can be used as stock dogs, these curs are widely-kept for hunting purposes in the southern area of the USA which is why they are also known as Southern curs.

Black mouth curs can be used to track a wide variety of game, including bears, although with small quarry, they may catch and overpower the creature on their own. These curs are very quiet when on the trail although they will certainly make a noise having sighted their quarry, as well as after treeing a raccoon for example.

Another out of the five types of 'mountain' cur which shows predominantly hunting rather than herding instincts is the treeing Tennessee brindle. It is thought to be descended from a combination of cur blood combined with Plott hound stock, with the brindle coloration of these hounds being a distinctive feature. A few have areas of black surrounded by brindle areas with odd patches of white present in some cases on their breast and feet. Treeing Tennessee brindles are relatively small in size, with their height varying between 12–24in (40–61cm), while their weight generally falls between 40–50lb (18–22.5kg).

They are easy hounds to care for and their size has seen them become increasingly popular as pets, as well as working companions. Treeing Tennessee brindles are now more common than ever, with the breed association having members in more than 30 states. As hounds, they have

Treeing Tennessee brindle. The brindle coloration of these hounds is reflected in their name, as is their state of origin.

Treeing Tennessee brindles have become very popular over recent years, thanks in part to their friendly temperament.

been kept to hunt raccoons, squirrels and possums, possessing keen scenting skills and excellent treeing abilities. Intelligent by nature, the treeing Tennessee brindle is a highly responsive dog, although it is sensitive and, like other hounds, requires a very positive training regimen. Persistent scolding can undermine its confidence.

The Stephens cur is just slightly smaller than its Tennessee neighbour, measuring up to 23in (59cm) in height, although it tends to be stockier, weighing as much as 55lb (25kg). These curs have been bred by the Stephens family in south-east Kentucky for over a century, being originally known as little blacks. It was not until 1970 however, that they became known under their present name of Stephens stock, reflecting the essential role played by this family in their development. They too have keen scenting skills, being able to pursue a cold trail and are usually pitted against raccoons and squirrels.

The Stephens stock is sometimes bred in colours other than the traditional black form, but this is unusual. Raccoons and squirrels are again their usual quarry, although they are quite capable of trailing larger game, even bears. The Stephens cur is a talented tracker, with the ability to follow cold trails. These hounds keep in touch well, not only when working the trail, but also once they have treed their quarry. They are very active hounds, in spite of their small size, and so are not really suitable as ordinary household companions, particularly in urban areas, in spite of their loyal, protective nature.

Mountain curs are very effective 'treers' of game, and are brave by nature when hunting.

Mountain curs have good pace. The natural bobtail of this particular dog is highlighted by its white tip.

The short coat of the mountain cur is usually yellow in colour, as in this instance.

Black-and-tan coonhound. Black coloration predominates in these particular coonhounds.

The American coonhounds share a common ancestry, which can be traced back to the American foxhound. Differences have arisen thanks to crosses involving other hound breeds, such as the bloodhound, whose influence is still clearly visible in the oldest of these breeds, which is the American black and tan coonhound.

The ancestry of this breed dates back to the late 18th century, when it was first used in the vicinity of the Ohio valley, by the Poe brothers. These hounds were highly valued for tracking purposes, being well-suited to following a cold trail.

The coonhound lineage developed by the Poes and then Simon Shirk and his grandson, Holmes Lingo, during the early years of the 1800s ultimately gave rise to the famous Old Glory strain. This pedigree remained dominant in the breed for over 130 years, attaining an unrivalled reputation.

The official registration bodies such as the American Kennel Club (AKC) refused to register coonhounds separately however, simply regarding them as foxhounds because of their ancestry. This was in spite of the fact that a variety of other breeds, including the Kerry beagle in this case, had contributed to their development. Finally, the United Kennel Club (UKC) recognised the American black-and-tan coonhound during 1900.

As its name suggests, this breed occurs only in a black-and-tan combination, with tan predominantly on the points. There should also be two characteristic pumpkin-seed shaped areas of tan above the eyes, with the coat itself being short, glossy and dense. On occasions however, some of these coonhounds show traces of white, most frequently on the chest.

Even today, the American black-and-tan coonhound is still kept predominantly as a working hound, rather than a show dog. Power and stamina are vital considerations in this respect, with the result that those used for hunting are invariably more muscular than their show ring counterparts.

Raccoons are their major quarry, although the coonhounds will also pursue opossum, with their scenting skills enabling them to track much bigger game, including wild boar and pumas. Since raccoons are essentially nocturnal animals, American black-and-tan coonhounds often hunt at night, with their distinctive, far-carrying calls allowing their owners to follow their progress.

Once they have successfully treed the raccoon – driven it up a tree – their bugle-like vocalisations change, indicating a successful outcome to the chase. When hunting in small groups, the different intonations of these hounds enable the huntsmen to distinguish between them. Only when they have found a fresh trail however, does a coonhound start to bay.

The UKC today registers about 12,000 of these coonhounds annually, so they are certainly not a minority breed. It was in 1959 that the AKC finally recognised the breed, dropping the American prefix from its name however, which can be a source of confusion. Even now though, the number registered with the AKC is small, typically not exceeding 600 individuals annually, reflecting the much lower level of interest in showing rather than working these hounds.

The UKC remains the major coonhound registry in the USA, recognising five other breeds of treeing hound. The English coonhound has an ancestry which includes the Virginian foxhounds, which in turn were ultimately brought from England. It was originally called the English fox and coonhound, as a means of describing part of its hunting skills, at a time when all coonhounds (save for the American black-and-tan plus the redbone) were grouped under the title of 'English' during the early 1900s. This was in spite of the fact that some of these coonhounds were much slower in the field than others.

The sleek, slender appearance of the English coonhound reveals a speedy hound with sturdy limbs. Today, the coloration of the breed has tended to become predominantly red ticked – solid coppery-red patches broken by similar

English coonhound. In some cases, red ticking, where the red and white hairs are mixed, is more prominent than in others.

ABOVE : The description 'English' is a reflection of the hounds that contributed to the ancestry of this breed.

BELOW: Although red ticking is common in English coonhounds, a much wider range of colours exists.

speckling on a white ground colour. As a result, they are also sometimes described as the red tick coonhound, although they may be bred in a range of other colours as well, including colours associated with different coonhounds, such as blue tick and brindle.

In terms of appearance however, the slender build of the English coonhound is highly distinctive. It has considerable pace, as indicated by the slope of its back and its powerful shoulders, plus plenty of stamina. Originally pitted more frequently against foxes, these coonhounds now hunt raccoon on a regular basis, as well as pumas and even bears on occasions, revealing a decidedly courageous side to their natures.

The Redbone coonhound, as distinct from the red tick coonhound, is entirely red in colour, and is in fact the only solid coloured member of the group, although some individuals do have small areas of white hair, most commonly on the chest and legs. The name of this breed comes not from its coloration however, but from that of one of the original breeders, Peter Redbone.

In the early days, during the 1800s, the coloration of these hounds was much more variable than it is today, with distinctive bicolours in existence. There were those which were red with a black area over their backs, described as saddlebacks, and others with prominent white patches of hair. A few were black-and-tan, possibly suggesting a bloodhound involvement in the breed's past. The southern states of Tennessee and Georgia are where the Redbone coonhound was developed.

It was not until after 1900 that steps were taken to standardise the coloration of these coonhounds. Registration in this case came relatively late in 1940, although Redbones distinguished themselves in the company of other

Solid red coloration is a distinguishing feature of the Redbone coonhound, although some individuals show small traces of white hair as well.

ABOVE: The Redbone coonhound has a very keen nose and great stamina, as well as being able to swim well.

coonhounds. The most famous line of descent was from a dog called Midnight Flyer via his great-great grandson known as Jungle Jim, who had a lasting impact on the pedigrees of the breed, dying in 1950.

The attractive appearance of these coonhounds has since seen them being kept on a much wider basis today, both in North America and overseas. They are friendly dogs, with a keen sense of smell. Their short coats are smooth yet hard to the touch, and easy to keep in good condition, even if they become muddy. Allowing the mud to dry and then simply brushing it out of the coat will maintain the immaculate appearance of this coonhound.

The Plott hound is a much darker shade than the Redbone coonhound, and also tends to be generally smaller in size. It has a distinctive brindle coloration, reflecting its German hound ancestry. The breed evolved in the Great Smoky Mountains in the vicinity of North Carolina and Tennessee. The forerunners of the breed were brought to this region by a young German immigrant called Johannes Plott. These

BELOW: A litter of Redbone coonhound puppies. This breed is now starting to become popular outside the USA.

Redbone coonhounds are solidly-built, with powerful legs and a broad nose.

Hannoverischer schweisshunds gradually developed, following crosses with other hounds and curs, while retaining the distinctive brindled appearance of their ancestors. They started to be kept by other families, and acquired their names, although basically none of these hounds differed significantly from those kept by the Plotts.

Changes started to occur during the 1920s however, following the introduction of Blevins' hounds to the existing lineage. These hounds were tan in colour, with a black saddle. Up until this stage, the lighter shade of brindle tended to predominate in the case of Plott hounds and

Plott hound. A native American breed descended from hounds of Germanic origins.

others of similar lineage, such as the Cable hounds, named after the Cable family of Swain County. But the Blevins' blood led to the appearance of much darker brindles, some having a black saddle while others were almost entirely black, apart from brindling on the legs.

Gola Ferguson, who began these crosses with Blevins' hounds, produced two of the most famous of all Plott hounds, christened Boss and Tigre. They left an indelible mark on the development of the breed. Before long, the Plotts themselves were using these hounds as crosses and when the matter of registration of the breed was raised, there was even a suggestion that they might be called Ferguson hounds, but their ancestral origins were ultimately reflected in their official breed name.

Other strains of hounds were used to a lesser extent in the recent development of the Plott hound, apart from Blevins'. This legacy can still be seen in the case of greyish-blue individuals, descended from the blue Delch strain.

Although buckskins crop up occasionally in litters, they cannot be registered with the UKC. This is because such coloration derives from crosses with Redbone coonhounds. Breeders of Plott hounds are keen to ensure the maintenance of their traditional hunting skills; their hounds are part of the cold trailing group of coonhounds, as distinct from the quicker Redbone. Allowing

ABOVE: Brindle coloration tends to predominate in the case of the Plott hound, although some have a black saddle.

BELOW: Blue tick coonhound. A breed which has heavy black ticking often apparent among areas of white hair.

crosses of this type to proliferate within the breed could therefore alter its character significantly.

The blue tick coonhound is another of the slower breeds, although in recent years, the emphasis on foxhound type has undoubtedly led to the development of more pacy individuals. Perhaps not surprisingly, these coonhounds have emerged from the vicinity of Louisiana, an area settled by French immigrants to the New World. The input of French hound blood is very apparent in their coloration, tracing back to the grand bleu de Gascogne.

Both share the blue ticking, caused by a combination of individual blue and white hairs in the coat, with tan coloration predominating on the muzzle and localised above the eyes in the shape of pumpkin seeds, as well as being present on the feet. Those blue tick coonhounds bred in the region of the Ozark mountains are regarded as being closest in appearance to their French ancestors. Others have more input from the American black-and-tan coonhound in their recent past.

These older-style coonhounds suffered with the emergence of raccoon hunting competitions in the 1950s, when judging depended on the numbers of raccoons treed by individual hounds. Those which worked at a fast pace such as the Redbone coonhound were therefore at a considerable advantage over their slower rivals.

When the breed was first recognised during the previous decade it was permissible for a short time to allow blue ticked puppies in a litter to be registered separately from littermates of red ticked appearance, that were then considered to be English coonhounds. The coloration of the blue tick coonhound is not confined to this breed however, since blue ticked individuals are seen in the case of the latter breed as well.

Working of coonhounds is becoming increasingly professional in some quarters, notably in the case of hunts organised by the Professional Kennel Club (PKC), where it can cost 200 dollars to enter an event. The prize money is often equally large, being up to 50,000 dollars at some top events.

The hunts take place in groups comprised of three or four coonhounds and their handlers, known as casts. The hunt itself is led by a guide, who may also be a cast member and can last for three hours or so. Judges award both plus and minus points, based on the performance of the individual coonhounds – minus scores awarded for a hound wandering away or returning unexpectedly to the cast can have a real impact on the outcome. It is not just instinctive ability that is important therefore, but good training as well.

The treeing Walker coonhound is another of the faster breeds, evolved originally from Virginian foxhounds of English descent. Its name commemorates that of Thomas Walker, who was responsible for bringing these hounds to Virginia in 1742. In due course, the distinctive Walker hounds developed, and the breeding of the treeing Walker coonhound took place as the result of an individual mating during the 1800s.

A Walker hound was mated with a highly regarded dog, possibly a cur, that had been stolen. This laid the foundation for this coonhound breed, which was not officially recognised until 1945. These coonhounds still display a close similarity to foxhounds, as reflected by their coloration. Tricolours are preferred, but bicolours can also be registered, with white often predominating in their coats. This can make these hounds easier to spot during the course of a night hunt.

Treeing Walker coonhound. A lively breed, which is fast, thanks to the significant foxhound input to its ancestry.

Coonhounds are being fitted with special tracking collars in some areas, especially for night-time hunts.

Tricoloured individuals are preferred in the case of the treeing Walker coonhound, with the coat itself being short and glossy.

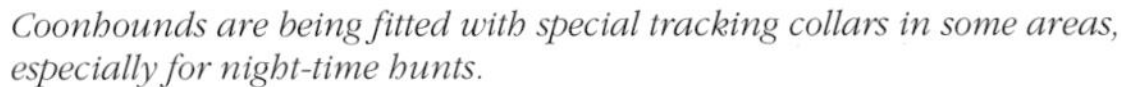

Treeing Walker coonhounds, which are a combination of tan and white, are never actually described as red-and-white although their tan coloration is similar to that of the Redbone coonhound. The term 'tan' is used to distinguish them. Not only are they able to hunt fast, but they also display good treeing ability.

The most recent addition to this group of hounds is the majestic tree hound. These are large and decidedly heavier than other coonhounds today, with bloodhounds having made a significant contribution to their ancestry. Male dogs are also much larger than their female counterparts. A breed association was first established for the majestic tree hound in 1980, with registrations also beginning during that year. These hounds can be bred in any colour or combination of colours, and have exceptional abilities to pick up on cold trails.

They were evolved to tackle larger quarry than raccoons, being pitted primarily against the bigger wild cats of the region, such as puma and bobcat, as well as bears. The origins of the breed grew out of a need to control the horse-killing activities of such cats in areas of the American south.

The American blue Gascon hound is another large and powerful breed, again related to the large French hound from the Gascony region. Not all display prominent tan markings. Unlike coonhounds, they actually pursue game on the ground, rather than treeing it. Foxes, wild boar and wolverines as well as wild cats can be the quarry of these hounds. It was thanks to a series of stories published by one of the most devoted aficionados of the breed, known as Wilson 'Blue tick Bill' Harshman, that it acquired its alternative name of Big 'n' Blue, based on the title of his book.

None of the hounds kept for hunting purposes early in history in Central and South America survive today as recognised breeds. Relatively few breeds have in fact originated from this part of the world, possibly because grey wolves did not range widely into this region. Even so, the southern part of the continent is home to the most hound-like of the wild canids – the maned wolf (*Chrysocyon brachyurus*), which, in spite of its name, is more closely allied to foxes. It stands up to 29in (76cm) tall at the shoulder. The long,

Treeing feist. An American hunting dog which originates from crosses between small hounds and terriers.

Maned wolves are the largest of the wild canids in South America, but have never been domesticated.

slender legs of the maned wolf provide good visibility in the grasslands of the pampas region, as well as giving valuable stride length when running.

The native hounds of South America are actually descended directly from European or American breeds, being of relatively recent origin. The Dogo Argentino, or Argentine mastiff, is probably the best-known, being developed during the 1920s in Argentina by Dr Antonio Martinez. He sought to create a breed which would be strong enough to overpower large, dangerous creatures such as puma and wild boar, while also proving to be a trustworthy and loyal guardian around the home. Dr Martinez used a variety of breeds including Spanish mastiff, bulldog and

Part mastiff, part hound, the Dogo Argentino's ears are often cropped in countries where this is permitted, to make the dogs look more fearsome.

boxer stock, in the form of the old fighting dog of Córdoba, as well as Irish wolfhounds among others for this purpose. After his death in 1956, his brother Agustin then continued the breeding programme.

The Dogo Argentino is a strong and powerful dog with a robust constitution, distinguished by its distinctive white coloration although some individuals have darker underlying spots on their skin. The coloration of their hair helps to reflect the heat, and assists the dogs to stay cool, especially when they are running. The temperament of the Dogo Argentino is generally sound, although this breed is actually banned from Britain under the *Dangerous Dogs Act*. In mainland Europe however, this breed has become increasingly popular, particularly in Germany and France, after being recognised for show purposes by the FCI in 1960.

These hybrid mastiff-hounds, presumably bearing some similarity to the old alaunt of medieval times, have served as police dogs, guide dogs for the blind and simply as loyal family companions. In its homeland, the Dogo Argentino hunts in packs, and in decided contrast to most hounds, they close in on their quarry without barking or baying in any way, so as to maintain what can be the critical element of surprise.

The Fila Brasileiro or Brazilian mastiff has a similar background to the Dogo Argentino, resulting from crossings between various mastiffs and bloodhounds. This ancestry is still clearly apparent in the breed today, as shown by its long muzzle and pronounced drooping ears, combined with loose facial folds of skin.

The description 'fila' derives from the Portuguese word meaning 'to hold'. When it was first bred during the 1800s, the Fila Brasileiro was used both in manhunts, tracking down escaped slaves, and also for rounding up farmstock, notably cattle which were allowed to roam in a state of semi-liberty. The cattle were seized and restrained by their ears, so they could be roped and penned in due course.

The Fila Brasileiro is an agile dog, in spite of its large size. It can run relatively fast, in a unique way, rocking from side to side as it moves, not unlike a camel, and also jumps well when necessary. In terms of temperament, this is a breed which requires firm training, and although such dogs are well-disposed to those whom they know well, strangers often arouse their aggressive instincts, whether or not this may be justified. Outside its homeland, the Fila Brasileiro is probably better known in North America than Europe at the present time.

In contrast, the other of Brazil's native breeds has a pure hound ancestry, being created from a combination of American foxhound and various coonhound crosses. The Rastreador Brasileiro shares the physical characteristics of the breeds that contributed to its development, having pendulous ears and a relatively long head. One of the most striking features is its yellow eyes. Its coloration reflects that of its ancestors, being a combination of white and other colours such as black, brown and blue, with the latter revealing a link back to the blue tick coonhound. The coat itself is short, with a rough texture.

Also known as the Brazilian tracker, this breed was developed essentially for hunting jaguar by Oswalde Aranha Filho. Stamina was a key requirement, with these hounds having to follow the scent of their quarry for seven hours or more, often through difficult terrain. Today, the Rastreador Brasileiro still remains rare, even in its homeland, although these hounds have a justified reputation for their friendly natures.

Typical Heights & Weights of Hound Breeds

AFGHANISTAN
Afghan hound 25-29in (64-74cm); 50-60lb (23-27kg)
ARABIA
Saluki 22-28in (56-71cm); 44-66lb (20-30kg)
ARGENTINA
Dogo Argentino 24-27in (61-69cm); 80-100lb (36-45kg)
AUSTRALIA
Kangaroo hound 27-30in (69-76cm); 60-70lb (27-32kg)
AUSTRIA
Alpenlandischer dachsbracke 13-16.5in (34-42cm); 33-40lb (15-18kg)
Austrian brandlbracke 18-23in (46-59cm); 44-50lb (20-23kg)
Peintinger bracke 17-23in (44-58cm); 33-40lb (15-18kg)
Tyroler bracke 17-19in (44-48cm); 33-48lb (15-21.5kg)
BRAZIL
Fila Brasileiro 24-30in (61-76cm); 90-110lb (41-50kg)
Rastreador Brasileiro 25-27in (63-69cm); 50-60lb (22-27kg)
CANADA
Tahltan bear dog 12-15in (31-38cm); 13-15lb (6-7kg)
CANARY ISLANDS
Canary Islands hound 22.5-27.5in (57-70cm); 42-55lb (19-25kg)
CONGO
Basenji 16-17in (41-43cm); 21-24lb (9.5-11kg)
DENMARK
Strellufstöver 12-15in (30-38cm); 35-40lb (16-18kg)
ESTONIA
Gontchaja Estonskaja 18-21in (46-53cm); 44-55lb (20-25kg)
FINLAND
Finnish hound 22-24,5in (56-62cm); 55lb (25kg)
FRANCE
Anglo-Français 24-28in (62-72cm); 76-78lb (34.5-35kg)
Ariegeois 21-24in (53-61cm); 55-66lb (25-30kg)
Basset Artésian Normand 10-14in (25-36cm); 33lb (15kg)
Basset bleu de Gascogne 13-16in (34-42cm); 35-40lb (16-18kg)
Basset fauve de Bretagne 13-15in (33-38cm); 35-40lb (16-18kg)
Beagle harrier 18-20in (45-50cm); 44-55lb (20-25kg)
Billy 24-26in (61-66cm); 55-66lb (25-30kg)
Briquet griffon Vendéen 19-22in (48-56cm); 50-53lb; (23-24kg)
Chien d'Artois 20.5-23in (52-58cm); 40-53lb (18-24kg)
Français tricolore 25.5-28in (65-72cm); 76-78lb (34.5-35.5kg)
Français blanc et noir 25.5-28in (65-72cm); 76-78lb (34.5-35.5kg)
Grand basset griffon Vendéen 15-16.5in (38-42cm); 40-44lb (18-20kg)
Grand bleu de Gascogne 25-28in (64-71cm); 71-77lb (32-35kg)
Grand Gascon-Saintongeois 25-28in (63-71cm); 66-71lb (30-32kg)
Grand griffon Vendéen 23.5-26in (60-66cm); 66-77lb (30-35kg)
Griffon fauve de Bretagne 20-22in (51-56cm) 44lb (20kg)
Griffon Nivernais 21-24in (53-62cm); 50-55lb (23-25kg)
Petit basset griffon Vendéen 13-15in (34-38cm); 31-40lb (14-18kg)
Petit bleu de Gascogne 20-23in (50-60cm); 40-48lb (18-22kg)
Petit Gascon-Saintongeois 23-25in (50-65cm); 60-66lb (27-30kg)
Petit griffon bleu de Gascogne 17-21in (43-52cm); 40-42lb (18-19kg)
Poitevin 24-28in (61-71cm); 62-66lb (28-30kg)
Porcelaine 22-23in (56-58cm); 55-62lb (25-28kg)
GERMANY
Deutsche bracke 16-21in (40-53cm); 45-50lb (20-22.5kg)
Bavarian schweisshund 20in (51cm); 55-77lb (25-35kg)
Hanoverian schweisshund 20-24in (51-61cm); 84-99lb (38-44kg)
Miniature dachshunds 5in (13cm); 9lb (4kg)
Standard dachshunds 9in (23cm); 10lb (5kg)
Westphalian dachsbracke 12-14in (30-36cm); 35-40lb (16-18kg)
GREAT BRITAIN
Basset hound 13-15in (33-38cm); 40-60lb (18-27kg)
Beagle 13-16in (33-41cm); 18-30lb (8-14kg)
Bloodhound 23-27in (58-69cm); 80-90lb (36-41kg)
Deerhound 28-30in (71-76cm); 80-100lb (36-45kg)
Fell hound 20-22in (51-56cm); 48-55lb (22-25kg)
Foxhound 23-27in (58-69cm); 55-75lb (25-34kg)
Greyhound 27-30in (69-76cm); 60-70lb (27-32kg)
Harrier 18-22in (46-56cm); 48-60lb (22-27kg)
Longdog - dependent on ancestry
Lurcher - dependent on ancestry
Otterhound 23-27in (58-69cm); 65-120lb (30-55kg)
Staghound 27-30in (69-76cm); 60-70lb (27-32kg)
Welsh hound 18-22in (46-56cm); 40lb (18kg)
Whippet 17-20in (43-51cm); 28lb (13kg)
GREECE
Greek greyhound 22-28in (56-71cm); 44-66lb (20-30kg)
Hellenic hound 18-22in (46-56cm); 38-44lb (17-20kg)
HUNGARY
Hungarian greyhound 25-27.5in (64-70cm); 49-68lb (22-31kg)
Transylvanian hound - short 18-20in (45-50cm); 48-55lb (22-25kg)
Transylvanian hound - tall 22-26in (56-66cm); 66-77lb (30-35kg)
IBIZA
Ibizan hound 22.5-27.5in (57-70cm); 42-55lb (19-35kg)
INDIA
Banjara greyhound 25.5-28.5in (65-71cm); 50-66lb (22.5-30kg)
Mahratta greyhound 22-30in (56-76cm); 51-70.5lb (23-32kg)
Rampur greyhound 25.5-28.5in (65-71cm); 50-66lb (22.5-30kg)
IRELAND
Irish wolfhound 28-35in (71-90cm); 90-120lb (40-55kg)
Kerry beagle 22-26in (56-66cm); 45-60lb (20-27kg)
ITALY
Italian greyhound 13-15in (33-38cm); 8lb (3.6kg)
Italian hound 20.5-23in (52-58cm); 40-62lb (18-28kg)
LATVIA
Latvian hound 16-19in (41-48cm); 30-40lb (14-18kg)
LITHUANIA
Lithuanian hound 21-24in (53-61cm); 55-62lb (25-28kg)
MAJORCA
Mallorquin 22.5-27.5in (57-70cm); 42-55lb (19-25kg)
MALI
Azawakh 23-29in (58-74cm); 37-55lb (17-25kg)
MALTA & GOZO
Pharaoh hound 21-25in (53-64cm); 45-55lb (20-25kg)

MOROCCO
Sloughi 24-28.5in (61-72cm); 45-60lb (20-27kg)
NORWAY
Dunker 18.5-22.5in (47-57cm); 35-49lb (16-22kg)
Haldenstövare 20-25in (51-64cm); 45-60lb (20-27kg)
Hygenhund 18.5-23in (47-58cm); 44-53lb (20-24kg)
POLAND
Polish hound 22-26in (56-66cm); 55-71lb (25-32kg)
PORTUGAL
Podengo Portugueso grande 23-28in (58-71cm); 60-66lb (27-30kg)
Podengo Portugueso medio 15-22in (39-56cm); 35-44lb (16-20kg)
Podengo Portugueso pequeño 8-12in (20-31cm); 11-13lb (5-6kg)
RUSSIA
Borzoi 27-31in (69-79cm); 75-105lb (35-48kg)
Chortaj 25-26in (63-66cm); 55-60lb (25-27kg)
Russian harlequin hound 22-26in (56-66cm); 55-75lb (25-34kg)
Russian drab yellow hound 22-27in (56-69cm); 55-75lb (25-34kg)
SICILY
Sicilian hound 16.5-19.5in (42-50cm); 18-26lb (8-12kg)
SLOVAKIA
Slovakian hound 18-20in (46-51cm); 44-49lb (20-22kg)
SPAIN
Sabueso Español de Monte 22in (56cm); 50-55lb (22.5-25kg)
Sabueso Español Lebrero 20in (51cm); 45-50lb (20-22.5kg)
Spanish greyhound 26-28in (66-71cm); 60-66lb (27-30kg)
SWEDEN
Drever 11.5-16in (29-41cm); 33lb (15kg)
Hamiltonstövare 20-24in (51-61cm); 50-60lb (23-27kg)
Schillerstövare 21-22in (53-57cm); 40-53lb (18-24kg)
Smalandsstövare 18-20in (46-50cm); 33-40lb (15-18kg)
SWITZERLAND
Berner laufhund 18-23in (46-58cm); 34-44lb (15-20kg)
Berner neiderlaufhund 13-16in (33-41cm); 34-40lb (15-18.5kg)
Jura laufhund: bruno 18-23in (46-58cm); 34-44lb (15-20kg)
Jura laufhund: St. Hubert 18-23in (46-58cm); 34-44lb (15-20kg)
Luzerner laufhund 18-23in (46-58cm); 34-44lb (15-20kg)
Luzerner neiderlaufhund 13-16in (33-41cm); 34-40lb (15-18.5kg)
Schweizer laufhund 18-23in (46-58cm); 34-44lb (15-20kg)
Schweizer neiderlaufund 13-16in (33-41cm); 34-40lb (15-18.5kg)
THAILAND
Thai ridgeback 23-26in (58-66cm); 51-75lb (23-34kg)
USA
American black-and-tan coonhound 23-27in (58-69cm); 55-75lb (25-35kg)
American blue Gascon hound 32in (81cm); 110lb (50kg)
American foxhound 21-25in (53-64cm); 65-75lb (30-34kg)
Black mouth cur 16-25in (40-64cm); 40-95lb (18-43kg)
Blue tick coonhound 20-27in (51-69cm); 45-80lb (20-36kg)
Catahoula leopard dog 20-26in (51-66cm); 40-50lb (18-23kg)
English coonhound 21-27in (53-69cm); 40-65lb (18-30kg)
Leopard cur 20-25in (51-64cm); 45-77lb (20-35kg)
Majestic tree hound 31in (79cm); 100lb (45kg)
Plott hound 20-24in (51-61cm); 45-55lb (20-25kg)
Redbone coonhound 21-26in (53-66cm); 50-70lb (23-32kg)
Stephens cur 16-23in (40-59cm); 35-55lb (16-25kg)
Treeing Tennessee brindle 16-24in (40-61cm); 40-50lb (18-23kg)
Treeing Walker coonhound 20-27in (51-69cm); 50-70lb (23-32kg)
YUGOSLAVIA (former)
Balkanski gonič 17-21in (43-53cm); 44lb (20kg)
Bosnian rough-haired hound 18-22in (46-56cm); 35-53lb (16-24kg)
Istrian hound: resasti 21-24in (53-61cm); 38-53lb (17-24kg)
Istrian hound: kratkodlaki 18-21in (46-53cm); 35-50lb (16-23kg)
Posavski gonič 17-23in (43-59cm); 35-45lb (16-20kg)
Yugoslavian mountain hound 18-22in (46-56cm); 44-45lb (20-25kg)
Yugoslavian tricoloured hound 18-22in (46-56cm); 44-45lb (20-25kg)
ZIMBABWE
Rhodesian ridgeback 24-27in (61-69cm); 65-85lb (30-39kg)

NOTE: Male dogs tend to be larger in terms of size and proportionately heavier than bitches.

Selected Bibliography

Although a number of the titles listed below may be out of print, they can be obtained from booksellers specialising in the field of canine literature, or possibly from public libraries.

Alderton, David (1984) *The Dog*, Macdonald.
Alderton, David (1993) *Eyewitness Handbook: Dogs*, Dorling Kindersley.
Alderton, David (1994) *Foxes, Wolves and Wild Dogs of the World*, Blandford.
Clutton-Brook, Juliet (1987) *A Natural History of Domesticated Mammals*, Cambridge University Press.
Delaney, Ronald (1984) *Hounds and Terriers*, Blandford.
Fiennes, R. & A. (1968) *The Natural History of the Dog*, Weidenfeld & Nicolson.
Gilbey, Sir Walter (1979) *Hounds in Old Days*, Spur Publications.
Grandjean, Dominique (1997) *Encyclopedie du Chien*, Hatier.
Hancock, David (1990) *The Heritage of the Dog*, Nimrod Press
Harmar, Hilary (1968) *The Bloodhound*, W & G Foyle.
Harper, Don (1994) *Dogs*, Parragon.
Hubbard, C.L.B. (1948) *Dogs in Britain*, Macmillan.
Johnston, George & Ericson, Maria (1979) *Hounds of France*, Saiga Publishing.
Kennel Club (1989) *The Kennel Club's Illustrated Breed Standards*, The Bodley Head.
Nicholas, A.K. & Foy, M.A. (1987) *The Dachshund*, T.F.H.
Palmer, Joan (1994) *The Illustrated Encyclopedia of Dog Breeds*, Blandford.
Plummer, D. Brian (1995) *The Development of the Dog*, The Boydell Press.
Raveneau, Alain (1994) *Inventaires des Animaux Domestiques en France*, Eclectis.
Ritchie, Carson I.A. (1981) *The British Dog: Its History from Earliest Times*, Robert Hale, 1981.
Russell, J. (1960) *All about Gazehounds*, Pelham.
Shaw, Michael (1984) *The Modern Lurcher*, The Boydell Press.
Wilcox, B. & Walkowicz, C. (1989) *The Atlas of Dog Breeds of the World*, T.F.H.

INDEX

Bold denotes a photograph